PBY CATALINA
PILOT'S FLIGHT OPERATING INSTRUCTIONS

This manual is sold for historic research purposes only, as an entertainment. It is not intended to be used as part of an actual flight training program. No book can substitute for flight training by an authorized instructor. The licensing of pilots is overseen by organizations and authorities such as the FAA and CAA. Operating an aircraft without the proper license is a federal crime.

©2007-2010 Periscope Film LLC
All Rights Reserved
ISBN #978-1-935327-94-3   1-935327-94-1
www.PeriscopeFilm.com

THE CLASSIFICATION OF THIS PUBLICATION HAS BEEN
CHANGED FROM RESTRICTED TO UNCLASSIFIED.

AN 01-5MA-1

Pilot's Handbook
of
Flight Operating Instructions

NAVY MODEL
PBY-5A Airplanes

THIS PUBLICATION SUPERSEDES AN 01-5MA-1 DATED 5 JUNE 1944
REVISED 20 JANUARY 1945

PUBLISHED UNDER JOINT AUTHORITY OF THE COMMANDING GENERAL,
ARMY AIR FORCES, THE CHIEF OF THE BUREAU OF AERONAUTICS,
AND THE AIR COUNCIL OF THE UNITED KINGDOM

Appendix I of this publication shall not be carried in aircraft on combat missions or
when there is a reasonable chance of its falling into the hands of the enemy

NOTICE.—This document contains information affecting the national defense of the United States within the meaning of the Espionage Act, 50 U. S. C., 31 and 32, as amended. Its transmission or the revelation of its contents in any manner to an unauthorized person is prohibited by law.

THESE ARE SUPERSEDING OR SUPPLEMENTARY PAGES TO SAME PUBLICATION OF PREVIOUS DATE

Insert these pages into basic publication
Destroy superseded pages

RESTRICTED AN 01-5MA-1

Pilot's Handbook
of
Flight Operating Instructions

NAVY MODEL
PBY-5A Airplanes

THIS PUBLICATION SUPERSEDES AN 01-5MA-1 DATED 5 JUNE 1944
REVISED 20 JANUARY 1945

PUBLISHED UNDER JOINT AUTHORITY OF THE COMMANDING GENERAL,
ARMY AIR FORCES, THE CHIEF OF THE BUREAU OF AERONAUTICS,
AND THE AIR COUNCIL OF THE UNITED KINGDOM

Appendix I of this publication shall not be carried in aircraft on combat missions or when there is a reasonable chance of its falling into the hands of the enemy

NOTICE.—This document contains information affecting the national defense of the United States within the meaning of the Espionage Act, 50 U. S. C., 31 and 32, as amended. Its transmission or the revelation of its contents in any manner to an unauthorized person is prohibited by law.

1 August 1945
Revised 15 October 1948

RESTRICTED
AN 01-5MA-1

Reproduction of the information or illustrations contained in this publication is not permitted without specific approval of the issuing service. The policy for use of Classified Publications is established for the Air Force in AR 380-5 and for the Navy in Navy Regulations, Article 76.

---LIST OF REVISED PAGES ISSUED---

INSERT LATEST REVISED PAGES. DESTROY SUPERSEDED PAGES.

NOTE: The portion of the text affected by the current revision is indicated by a vertical line in the outer margins of the page.

Page No.	Latest Revised Date
14	15 October 1948

* The asterisk indicates pages revised, added or deleted by the current revision.

BuAer

ADDITIONAL COPIES OF THIS PUBLICATION MAY BE OBTAINED AS FOLLOWS:

USAF ACTIVITIES.—In accordance with Technical Order No. 00-5-2.
NAVY ACTIVITIES.—Submit request to nearest supply point listed below, using form NavAer-140: NAS. Alameda, Calif.; ASD. Orote, Guam: NAS. Jacksonville, Fla.; NAS. Norfolk, Va.; NASD. Pearl City, Oahu; NASD. Philadelphia, Pa.; NAS. San Diego, Calif.; NAS. Seattle, Wash.
For listing of available material and details of distribution see Naval Aeronautics Publications Index NavAer 00-500.

RESTRICTED

TABLE OF CONTENTS

Section	Page
I Description	
1. Airplane—General Arrangement	1
2. Arrangement of Operating Equipment and Controls	1
3. Landing Gear Operation	10
4. Float Gear Operation	12
5. Auxiliary Power Plant Operation	13
6. Central Heater System Operation	13
7. Wing and Tail Anti-Icer Operation	13
8. Propeller Anti-Icer Operation	14
9. Operation of Miscellaneous Equipment	14
10. Movement of Flight Personnel	15
II Pilot Operating Instructions	
1. Before Entering the Pilot's Compartment	37
2. On Entering the Pilot's Compartment	38
3. Fuel System Management	39
4. Starting Engines	45
5. Engine Warm-up and Accessory Check	46
6. Emergency Take-off	49
7. Engine and Accessories Operation Ground Test	49
8. Taxiing Instructions	49
9. Take-off	51
10. Engine Failure During Take-off	53
11. Climb and High Speed Level Flight	53
12. General Flying Characteristics	53
13. Maneuvers Prohibited	54
14. Stalls	54
15. Spins	54
16. Acrobatics	54
17. Diving	55
18. Night Flying	55
19. Approach and Landing	56
20. Stopping Engines	60
21. Before Leaving the Pilot's Compartment	60
III Flight Operating Data	
1. Specific Engine Flight Chart	61
2. Air Speed Limitations	61
3. Air Speed Calibration Chart	61
4. Balance Computer Designation	61
IV Emergency Operation	
1. Emergency Operation of Landing Gear	65
2. Emergency Operation of Floats	66
3. Emergency Take-off	68
4. Engine Failure During Take-off	68
5. Engine Failure During Landing	68
V Operational Equipment	
1. Remote Compartments	71
2. Operation of Oxygen System	71
3. Operation of Communications Equipment	72
4. Armament	83
Appendix I	
Flight Operating Charts, Tables, Curves and Diagrams	95

Three-Quarter Rear View

Three-Quarter Front View

SECTION I
DESCRIPTION

1. AIRPLANE—GENERAL ARRANGEMENT.

This airplane is an all-metal, two-engine amphibian, with a flying boat hull 63 feet-10 inches long, equipped with retractable tricycle type landing gear. It is powered by two Pratt and Whitney R-1830-92 engines.

Wing span is 104 feet. The wing is mounted on a superstructure built up from the hull, and is braced by four struts, two on each side, extending from the hull to the under surface of the wing. Wing main center and outer panels are aluminum alloy, beam and truss, stressed skin construction, with detachable trailing edges made of braced metal ribs covered with doped fabric. Leading edges of both center and outer panels are all metal, and are detachable. Main panel and leading and trailing edge structures incorporate ducts for the heat anti-icing system, which derives its heat from the engine exhaust. The wing also incorporates the engine nacelles, fuel and oil tanks and the two retractable auxiliary floats and their operating mechanism.

The two ailerons and their trailing edge fairings are constructed of braced metal ribs, fabric covered. The port aileron has a metal trim tab which may be adjusted by the pilot during flight.

The stern portion of the hull tapers to a point in a horizontal plane, and sweeps upward vertically to form a dorsal fin, which becomes the lower section of the vertical stabilizer. Horizontal stabilizer and upper part of the vertical stabilizer are bolted to the hull portion of the vertical stabilizer. The horizontal stabilizer is all metal except for its trailing edges, which are metal frames, fabric covered.

Rudder and elevator are also metal frames, fabric covered. Both rudder and elevators have metal trim tabs which may be adjusted by the pilot during flight.

The hull is divided into five main watertight compartments, separated by four main bulkheads equipped with watertight doors. The bomber's compartment is in the nose of the hull, and immediately aft of the bomber's compartment is the pilot's compartment, which extends aft as far as the first watertight bulkhead.

Radio operator's and navigator's compartment is aft of the pilot's compartment. Radio and radar operators occupy the starboard side of the compartment. The navigator is stationed on the port side of the same compartment. The engineer's station is in the superstructure which supports the wing. The compartment immediately below the engineer's station contains the galley stove, food locker, and auxiliary power unit. This compartment is narrow because of the indentations of the landing wheel wells. Crew quarters are aft of this galley compartment, and the gun blisters and tail compartment are aft of the crew's quarters.

2. ARRANGEMENT OF OPERATING EQUIPMENT AND CONTROLS.

a. PILOT'S COMPARTMENT.
(See figure 1.)

(1) SURFACE CONTROLS.—Dual surface controls are provided for pilot and co-pilot. Rudder control is in the form of two sets of pedals. Elevator control is in the form of a movable yoke, with its two vertical supports on either side of the cockpit, and a horizontal bar, parallel with the instrument panel, joining the tops of the two vertical members. Elevator control is achieved by moving the yoke forward or aft in the conventional control stick movements.

Aileron controls consist of two hand wheels mounted on the horizontal yoke bar at the pilot's and co-pilot's positions, and linked together by a chain and cable loop around sprockets.

Metal trim tabs are installed on rudders, elevators and the port aileron. The aileron tab is controlled by a knob at the bottom of the pilot's side of the main instrument panel. The rudder and elevator tab controls are located overhead in the ceiling of the pilot's compartment.

Elevator and aileron controls are locked by means of a detachable bar, one end of which is fitted against the pilot's aileron wheel in such a manner as to clamp the wheel in neutral position to the control yoke. The bar is strapped to the yoke and the yoke is pulled back until the opposite end of the locking bar meets a fitting, near the side of the hull, aft of the pilot's seat. When the bar is secured in this fitting, it holds the elevator control yoke in neutral position.

The rudder is locked by means of a hinged lever which pulls out from the side of the hull, just under the pilot's side window.

(2) LANDING GEAR CONTROLS.—Operating control for the hydraulic landing gear lowering and retracting mechanism consists of a small lever at the bottom of the main instrument panel on the pilot's side. Pedals to operate the landing wheel brakes are mounted on the tops of the rudder pedals. A parking brake setting knob is located at the bottom of the main instrument panel on the co-pilot's side. A hand pump to furnish pressure to the landing gear and brake systems in case of failure of the engine-driven hydraulic pump is located inboard of the co-pilot's seat, and is accessible to both pilots.

A selector valve allows a choice of liquids which the pump will furnish.

A Marquette electric windshield wiper is installed, with controls, in the ceiling of the pilot's compartment, aft of the tab controls.

(3) POWER PLANT CONTROLS. *(See figure 14.)*—The pilot's power plant controls consist of throttles, located in the ceiling of the pilot's compartment; propeller governor control levers, alongside the throttles; propeller feathering switches, ahead of the propeller governor levers; and ignition switches, on the elevator-aileron control yoke bar.

All other power plant controls are in the engineer's compartment.

(4) MISCELLANEOUS CONTROLS IN PILOT'S COMPARTMENT.

(a) WINDSHIELD SPRAY AND WIPER.— A hand pump with which to spray the windshields with either clean water or alcohol de-icing solution is located outboard of the instrument panel, on the co-pilot's side.

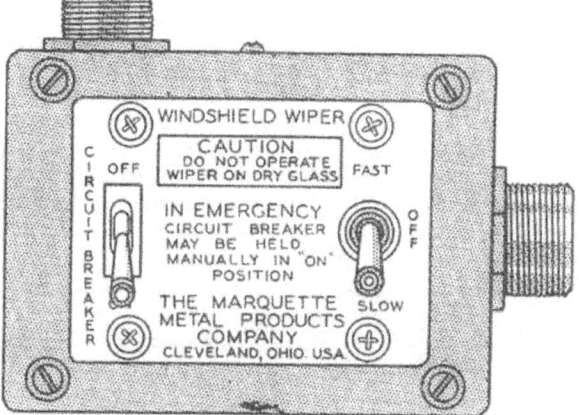

(b) PROPELLER AND WING ANTI-ICER CONTROLS.—A rheostat for controlling the speed and output of the propeller anti-icer pump is on the control yoke. Switches for controlling the hot air wing anti-icing equipment are also on the control yoke, next to the anti-icer rheostat.

(c) VACUUM PUMP SELECTOR VALVE.— A vacuum pump selector valve is located at the bottom of the instrument panel on the pilot's side. The valve may be set so that the righthand pump will run the gyropilot and the left-hand pump will run the directional gyro and gyro horizon; or so that the left-hand pump will run the gyropilot, and the right-hand pump will run the gyro instruments.

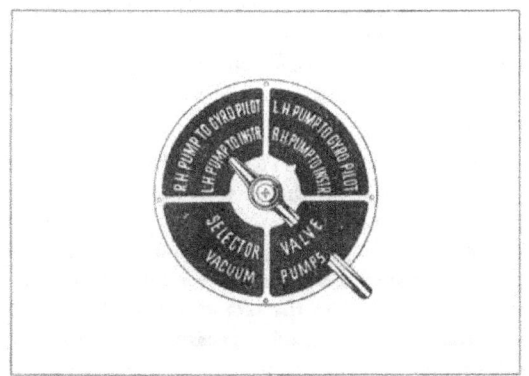

(d) GYROPILOT CONTROLS.—The Sperry Mark 3 gyropilot panel is in the center cut-out of the main instrument panel. The main four-way oil valve for the system is on the port side of the hull, just forward of the pilot's seat. The servo speed control valves are at the bottom of the gyro pilot panel. The "ON-OFF" control handle is over the bulkhead door, just aft of the pilot's seat. The bomb sight gyro transfer valve is at the bottom of the instrument panel, to the right of the vacuum pump selector valve.

(e) PILOT'S AND CO-PILOT'S SEAT ADJUSTMENTS.—The pilot's and co-pilot's seats may be adjusted for tilt and for fore-and-aft position by releasing spring-loaded locking pins controlled by levers on the outboard sides of the seats.

(f) RUDDER PEDAL ADJUSTMENT.—Both sets of rudder pedals may be adjusted for fore-and-aft position by releasing spring-loaded locking pins controlled by levers which may be moved with the feet. The levers are on the outboard side of each pedal.

(g) PILOT'S COMPARTMENT VENTILATION CONTROLS.—Openings in each side of the hull immediately aft of the instrument panel, provide for admission of fresh air during flight. These openings are closed with watertight hinged covers during take-offs and landings. Knobs controlling opening, closing and locking of the covers are within easy reach of the pilot and co-pilot. Pilot's and co-pilot's side windows have sliding panels which may be opened to obtain additional ventilation. The sliding panels may be latched in any position, open or closed.

(h) PILOT'S ELECTRIC SWITCH PANEL. (See figure 2.)—The pilot's electric switch panel over the bulkhead door, to the rear of the pilot's and co-pilot's seats, contains the bomb-torpedo firing key receptacle; the bomb-torpedo selector switch; the receptacle switch; the right-left torpedo release power switches; the pilot director indicator switch; the pitot head heater switch; the section light switches; anchor light switch; wing and tail light switches; formation light switches; landing light switches; warning horn button, and fluorescent and projector light switches.

(i) PILOT'S INTERPHONE CONTROL PANEL.—The pilot's interphone control panel is directly over the pilot's electric switch panel. The panel has a four-position selector switch, permitting the following combinations of radio-interphone hook-ups:

1. Co-pilot on interphone system and intrasquadron receiver; pilot on intrasquadron set only.

2. Co-pilot on intrasquadron set only; pilot on interphone system and intrasquadron receiver.

3. Both pilot and co-pilot on interphone system and intrasquadron receiver.

4. Both pilot and co-pilot on interphone system only.

Volume controls and alternate receiver switch are also on the interphone control panel.

Pilot's and co-pilot's interphone station boxes are on the sides of the hull, outboard of pilot's and co-pilot's seats.

A recall signal for the radio operator is placed on the interphone control panel, so that the radio operator may be called in case he has cut off the interphone circuit from his head set.

(j) RECOGNITION LIGHT SWITCHES AND KEY.—The recognition light switch and key box is mounted on the elevator-aileron control yoke.

(k) PILOT'S ATB/ARB CONTROLS.—Pilot's transmitter control unit for the ATB radio equipment is directly above the interphone control panel,

Section I
Paragraph 2

on the co-pilot's side of the bulkhead. Receiver switch box and remote tuning head for the ARB radio are located at approximately the same level, on the pilot's side of the bulkhead.

(l) PILOT'S RU-19 RECEIVER CONTROLS.—A switch box and remote tuner for the RU-19 radio receiving equipment are located on the pilot's side of the aft bulkhead, near the ARB control box and tuning head.

(m) MARKER BEACON.—The marker beacon switch and lights are on the pilot's side of the main instrument panel.

(n) EMERGENCY BOMB RELEASE HANDLES.—Emergency release handles for quick jettisoning of bombs from port and starboard wing racks are at the bottom of the main instrument panel, on either side of the passageway to the bomber's compartment.

(o) FLARE RELEASE HANDLES.—Flare release handles are directly over the center of the door in the aft bulkhead of the pilot's compartment.

(5) INSTRUMENTS IN PILOT'S COMPARTMENT.
(See figures 3 and 4.)

(a) FLIGHT AND NAVIGATION INSTRUMENTS.—The pilot has the following flight and navigation instruments on his side of the main instrument panel:

Altimeter
Air Speed Indicator
Directional Gyro
Gyro Horizon
Radio Altimeter
Turn and Bank Indicator
Rate of Climb Indicator
Remote Compass Indicator
Pilot Director Indicator

The co-pilot has the following flight and navigation instruments on his side of the main instrument panel:

Altimeter
Air Speed Indicator
Turn and Bank Indicator
Rate of Climb Indicator
Remote Compass Indicator
Pilot Director Indicator

The Mark 3 Sperry gyropilot control panel, located in the center of the main instrument panel, contains the following instruments:

Directional Gyro
Bank and Climb Indicator

(b) PILOT'S ENGINE INSTRUMENTS.—The pilot's tachometers, manifold pressure gages and engine speed synchronism indicator are in the center of the main instrument panel, above the Sperry Mark 3 gyropilot control unit.

(c) OTHER INSTRUMENTS AND INDICATING LIGHTS.—The suction gage and hydraulic fluid pressure gage for the Sperry Mark 3 gyropilot system are on the system control panel, in the center of the main instrument panel. The marker beacon light is on the main panel to the left of the gyropilot panel. The landing gear hydraulic pressure gage is on the co-pilot's side of the main instrument panel.

Landing gear up and down latch indicator lights are on the co-pilot's side of the instrument panel.

(d) PILOT-ENGINEER SIGNAL SYSTEM. *(See figures 5 and 20.)*—In addition to the interphone system, a system of signal lights is provided to enable the pilot to transmit orders to the engineer concerning operation of certain controls not available to the pilot. The system consists of duplicate sets of nine lights operated by individual single pole, single throw toggle switches, on the pilot's control yoke and the engineer's instrument panel. These lights are behind small ground-glass windows and the windows are lettered as follows; "RAISE FLOATS," "LOWER FLOATS," "FULL RICH," "AUTO RICH," "AUTO LEAN," "STOP ENGINES," "RECALL," "INTERPHONE," and "SECURE." The pilot may signal the engineer to perform any of the above operations by switching the proper light on. The engineer may acknowledge the order by switching the light off. The light marked "INTERPHONE" on either panel indicates that either pilot or engineer desires to talk to the other on the interphone system.

b. ENGINEER'S COMPARTMENT.

(1) POWER PLANT, FUEL AND OIL SYSTEM CONTROLS.—The carburetor mixture control levers and quadrant are located above the center of the engineer's instrument panel, between the fuel flowmeter.

The alternate carburetor air intake control handles are on the engineer's instrument panel, on either side of the electrical switch panel.

The cowl flap hand cranks are on the instrument panel bulkhead, below the panel.

Engine starter and inertia meshing switches are on the left side of the electrical switch panel.

Emergency fuel pump (wobble pump) handles are at the top center of the engineer's instrument panel, above the electrical switch panel and below the fuel flowmeters.

AN 01-5MA-1

Figure 1 – General View of Pilot's Compartment Showing Controls Locked

Section I
Paragraph 2

AN 01-5MA-1

Figure 2—Pilot's Communication and Electrical Controls

Engine primer is immediately below the port window of the engineer's compartment.

Fuel tank selector valves are on either side of the instrument panel, under the carburetor air control handles.

The fuel cross-feed valve, used only in case of a fuel pump failure, is at the lower left corner of the instrument panel.

The fuel strainer drain valves are on either side of the instrument panel, the left-hand drain valve being immediately above the cross-feed valve, and the right-hand valve in the bottom right-hand corner of the instrument panel.

The auxiliary power plant fuel valve is on the right-hand side of the instrument panel, just above the right-hand strainer drain valve. This valve also furnishes fuel to the tail de-icing unit.

Fuel tank drain valves are on either side of the upper part of the engineer's compartment, aft of the engineer's seat.

Fuel sight gage shut-off valves are on the bottoms of all sight gages.

Fuel dump valves are in the top of the engineer's compartment, directly above his seat.

Fuel tank vapor dilution system handle is just aft of the starboard window, at the rear of the engineer's seat.

By-pass control handles for the fuel flowmeters are on the bottoms of the flowmeters.

A diagram of the airplane fuel system, indicating how the fuel valves should be operated, is mounted on a card just ahead of the port window.

Oil dilution control switches are on the electrical switch panel. Oil gage energizer and selector switches are on the same panel, to the left of the oil dilution switches.

(2) AUXILIARY POWER PLANT CONTROLS.—The auxiliary power unit is on the starboard side of the galley, which is immediately below the engineer's station, and between the same two bulkheads. This auxiliary power unit is an Eclipse, Type NEP-2 auxiliary power plant engine driving a Type NEB-1D generator. The engine also drives a small bilge pump.

The engine is started manually, by means of a rope wrapped around the starting pulley.

6

AN 01-5MA-1

Section I

Figure 3—Pilot's Instrument Panel

Figure 4—Co-pilot's Instrument Panel

Section I
Paragraph 2
AN 01-5MA-1

A two-position choke lever is mounted on the carburetor intake at the aft end of the engine. A grounding switch button is located on the side of the magneto, also at the aft end of the engine. These are the only engine controls.

The fuel supply is turned on by the selector valve at the bottom of the engineer's instrument panel.

(3) ENGINE, FUEL AND OIL SYSTEM INSTRUMENTS. *(See figure 5.)*—Engineer's engine instruments consist of two manifold pressure gages, two engine cylinder temperature gages and two tachometers. Oil system instruments consist of an oil quantity gage (liquidometer) and two oil temperature and pressure gages, incorporated as parts of the engine gage units. Fuel system instruments consist of fuel pressure gages incorporated as parts of the engine gage units; fuel flowmeters; quantity sight gages; and an inclinometer and tilt charts to be used in conjunction with the sight gages.

Manifold pressure gages, tachometers and the engine gage units, incorporating oil temperature and pressure and fuel pressure gages, are at the bottom of the engineer's instrument panel. The cylinder temperature gages and the oil quantity gage (liquidometer) are directly above the manifold pressure gages, tachometer, etc. The two fuel flowmeters are at the top of the engineer's instrument panel. Fuel sight gages are in two sets, one just aft of the flowmeters and one aft of the engineer's seat. The inclinometer, for determining the longitudinal angle of the airplane, is just aft of the bottom of the instrument panel near the starboard side window. The tilt charts which interpret the sight gage readings at various angles are located above the starboard side window.

(4) ADDITIONAL INSTRUMENTS, INDICATORS AND CONTROLS IN ENGINEER'S COMPARTMENT.—Temperature indicators for the hot air wing and tail anti-icing system are located on the port side wall of the engineer's compartment, just outboard of the engineer's seat.

The float operating switch and warning light are

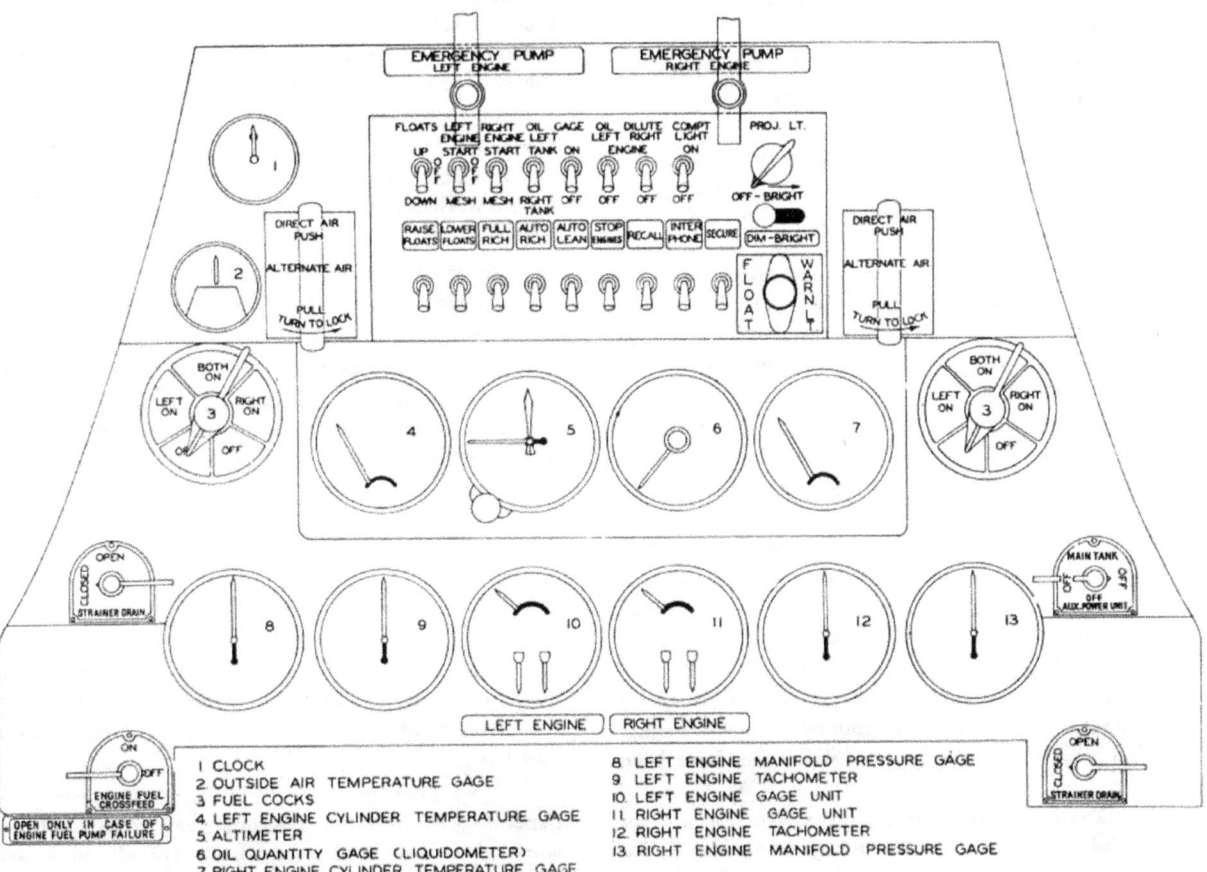

1 CLOCK
2 OUTSIDE AIR TEMPERATURE GAGE
3 FUEL COCKS
4 LEFT ENGINE CYLINDER TEMPERATURE GAGE
5 ALTIMETER
6 OIL QUANTITY GAGE (LIQUIDOMETER)
7 RIGHT ENGINE CYLINDER TEMPERATURE GAGE
8 LEFT ENGINE MANIFOLD PRESSURE GAGE
9 LEFT ENGINE TACHOMETER
10 LEFT ENGINE GAGE UNIT
11 RIGHT ENGINE GAGE UNIT
12 RIGHT ENGINE TACHOMETER
13 RIGHT ENGINE MANIFOLD PRESSURE GAGE

Figure 5—Engineer's Instrument Panel

on the electrical switch panel, on the engineer's instrument panel.

A clock and outside air thermometer are located on the port side of the instrument panel.

An altimeter is installed on the instrument panel, between the port engine cylinder temperature gage and the oil quantity gage.

Pilot-engineer signal system lights and switches are at the bottom of the electrical switch panel on the engineer's instrument panel.

c. CONTROLS IN RADIO OPERATOR-NAVIGATOR'S COMPARTMENT.—The radio operator-navigator's compartment is immediately aft of the pilot's compartment and forward of the engineer's compartment. Besides the radio operator's and navigator's equipment, the compartment contains the airplane central heating unit and the main power distribution, radio, interphone and radar equipment control panels.

The navigator's station is on the port side of the compartment. The radio operator's table and seat are on the starboard side. The radar operator's table and seat are on the starboard side forward of the radio operator's station.

(1) MAIN POWER DISTRIBUTION PANEL. *(See figure 18.)*—The main power distribution panel is located on the starboard side of the compartment on the bulkhead, aft of the radio operator's table. The panel contains the main and auxiliary battery ammeters; the main and auxiliary generator ammeters; the voltmeter and its selector switch; bus selector switches for main and auxiliary generators and batteries; and bus selector or line switches for all the electrically operated equipment on the airplane, except radio. Th radio d-c power switch is immediately below the distribution panel.

(2) AIRPLANE CENTRAL HEATER SYSTEM.—The heating unit for the airplane central heater system is installed under the navigator's table. Damper for the control of intake air for the system is in the intake duct on the port side of the hull, in the radio operator-navigator's compartment.

The dampers for directing the flow of heated air fore-and-aft in the ship are in the "Y" fitting immediately above the central heater unit.

All damper controls consist of simple levers with knobs for handles, and thumb screws or spring-loaded pins to hold positions for which they have been set.

The switch for turning the system on and off is on the control box over the navigator's table. A line switch and fuse are on the main power distribution panel.

d. CREW'S QUARTERS.—The crew compartment is immediately aft of the radio operator-navigator's compartment. This compartment contains three bunks. Two bunks are located one above the other on the starboard side. A smoke tank release handle is located on the forward bulkhead, over the door.

e. WAIST GUN COMPARTMENT. *(See figure 55.)*—The waist gun compartment is aft of the crew compartment, and contains the two .50 caliber waist guns, with their ammunition stowage box and feed chutes. Camera power receptacles are provided at each gun station, for plugging in the N-4 cameras, when installed.

Control switches for the camera receptacle ammunition feed boosters and the Mark 9 Illuminated Gun Sight for the side waist guns are on either side of the compartment just ahead of the gun positions.

The compartment is enclosed on both sides by large transparent streamlined blisters, each of which pivots on a horizontal fore-and-aft axis, so that it may be opened to allow for firing the guns. When closed, the blisters are kept watertight by inflatable sealing tubes. A valve for releasing the air in the sealing tubes is integral with each latch. A hand pump for inflating the sealing tubes is stowed aft of the port blister. Instructions for operating the waterseals are on both sides of the aft bulkhead.

Brackets for mounting an astro-compass, for use by the navigator, are mounted at forward end of each blister.

Air scoop pull handle and control switch for the tail anti-icing heater are on the aft bulkhead, over the doorway.

f. TAIL COMPARTMENT.—The tail compartment extends from the aft bulkhead of the waist gun compartment to the tail of the ship, and contains the flare release tubes and the tunnel gun and camera hatch. No operating controls are in the tail compartment.

3. LANDING GEAR OPERATION.

a. NORMAL OPERATION.

(1) TO LOWER GEAR.

(a) Turn selector valve handle *(See figure 3.)* on pilot's panel to "DOWN" position. See that lever safety catch clicks into place, locking lever in down position.

(b) Turn indicator light switch on instrument panel to "W" position. Landing gear down light will show when main and nose wheels are all down and latched. As pilot cuts throttle to below 15 inches Hg manifold pressure, the float warning lights on both

Section I

AN 01-5MA-1

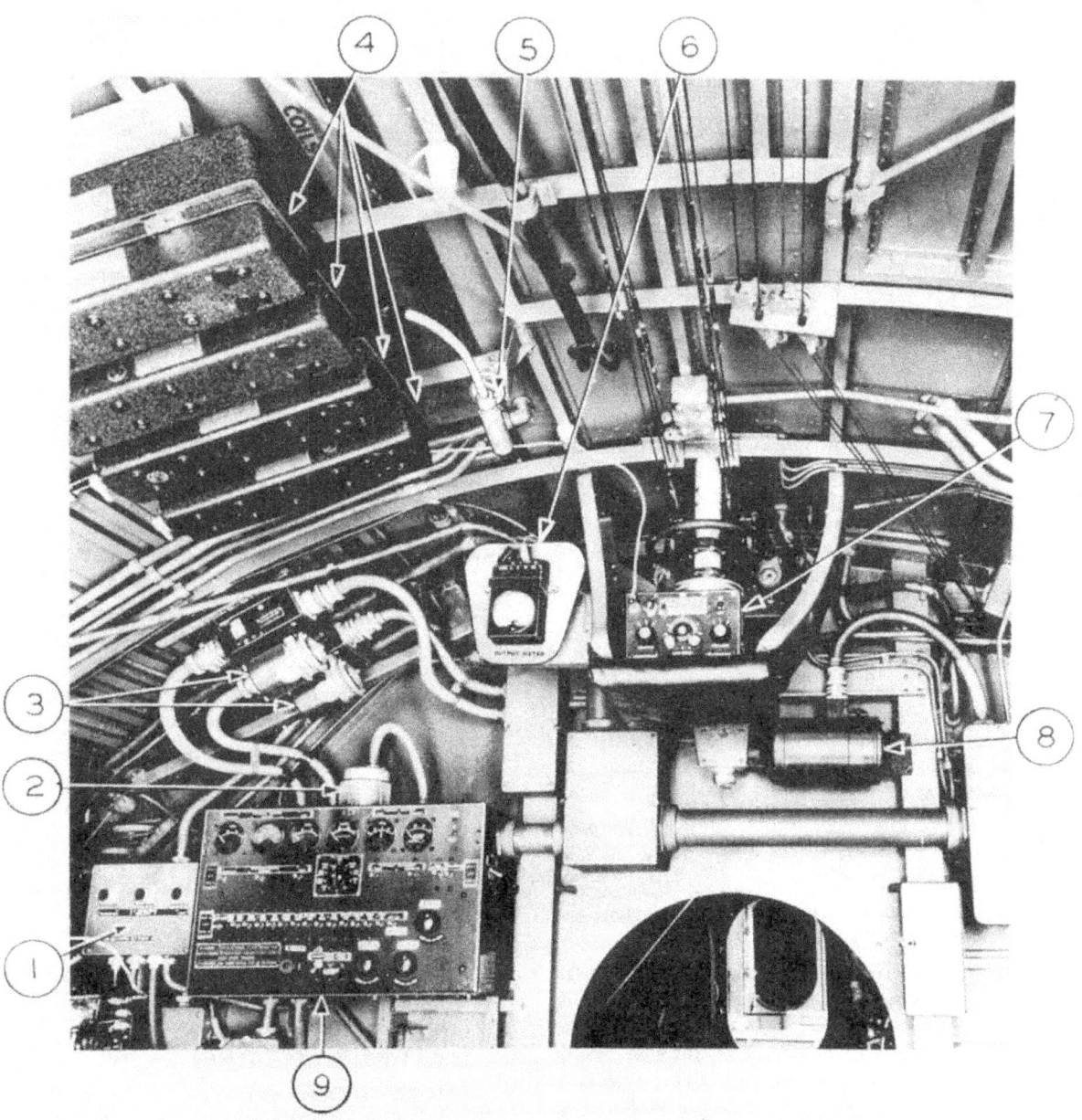

1. A-C Distribution Panel
2. Oil Quantity Gage Voltage Compensator
3. Engine Generator D-C Voltage Regulators
4. RU-19 Spare Tuning Coils
5. Radio Compartment Projector Light
6. DW-2 Output Meter
7. DW-2 Receiver
8. Float Control Motor
9. Main Distribution Panel

Figure 6—Equipment on Forward Face of Bulkhead 4

Section I
Paragraph 3-4

AN 01-5MA-1

engineer's and pilot's panels will show, indicating that the floats are up.

(2) TO RAISE GEAR.

(a) Loosen safety catch on landing gear control lever.

(b) Raise lever to "UP" position.

(c) The two lights indicating "Main Landing Gear Up" and "Nose Wheel Door Locked" will not show until the main wheels are both securely latched and the nose wheel doors are closed and latched.

CAUTION

Gear control lever must be either full up or full down at all times. Do not allow it to remain in any intermediate position.

b. EMERGENCY OPERATION. *(See figures 40 and 44.)*—If landing gear failure is due to failure of starboard engine or engine-driven hydraulic pump, and not to loss of fluid caused by leaking reservoir or lines, the gear may be lowered with pressure supplied by the hand pump. Latch the control handle in "DOWN" position before operating pump. Be sure to check "Gear Down and Latched" with indicator lights.

If starboard engine and hydraulic pump are running and gear fails to lower when handle is pushed down, check hydraulic pressure gage. If gage shows above 1000 lb pressure, return handle to up position and repeat attempt to lower gear. If gear does not lower on second attempt, leave gear handle locked in down position and:

(1) Release the main wheel up locks by pulling out the "T" handles at the main wheel wells and turning handles ¼ turn.

(2) Work gear down by rocking the airplane approximately 14° to each side.

(3) Use the emergency "DOWN-LATCH" lever to straighten out the main support struts and latch the gear in the down position. To do this, first insert emergency "DOWN-LATCH" lever through access door provided inside of wheel well, and engage the handle end of the lever over the bolt provided on the auxiliary keel. With handle end of lever supported by the bolt, guide the outboard end of the lever into the strut socket, located immediately above the pivot point in the strut.

(4) Push firmly on the lever to straighten out the strut and gear will latch down. Repeat same operation for gear on opposite side.

(5) Unlock nose wheel doors by pushing door lock handle aft, (located on the starboard side, forward of bulkhead 1) thus releasing the door lockpins.

(6) Insert hydraulic hand pump handle or emergency "DOWN-LATCH" lever handle in the aft end of the starboard door torque tube, (located aft of bulkhead 2) and push inboard, (counterclockwise), rotating the torque tube and thus opening the nose wheel well doors.

Note

In airplanes where the radar antennae have been installed, it will not be possible to use the emergency "DOWN-LATCH" lever for emergency manual operation of the nose wheel doors. However, the hydraulic hand pump handle may be substituted for this purpose.

(7) Lock torque tube in "DOORS OPEN" position by swinging locking link inboard over the lug on the torque tube end fitting. Insert lockpin and retain with safety pin.

(8) Remove aft nose wheel cover plug and insert emergency lever through the hole. Strike the end of the up-latch sharply to unlatch the nose gear.

(9) Attach the emergency lever to the torque tube between the packing nut and the jack fitting, so that the ratchet pawl fits into the teeth of the jack fitting. Using the lever as a ratchet, force the gear into the down position. To lock, use a slow, heavy push.

(10) Remove the forward plug of the wheel well cover to examine the down-latch and use emergency "DOWN-LATCH" lever to determine if the down-latch is locked. If it is locked, the red collar on the lever will not extend above the hole in the cover, and the oleo strut will be vertical and against the down bumper.

CAUTION

Before operating gear again, be sure to release the emergency door lockpin.

4. FLOAT GEAR OPERATION.

a. NORMAL OPERATION.
(See figures 5 and 17.)

(1) TO LOWER FLOATS.

(a) Turn float switch on engineer's instrument panel to "FLOATS DOWN" position.

(b) If throttles are retarded to 15 inches Hg manifold pressure, the float warning lights on pilot's and engineer's instrument panels will go on until floats are down and latched. The wheel indicator lights will show "MAIN LANDING GEAR UP" and "NOSE WHEEL DOOR LOCKED."

(c) Do not begin to lower floats at speeds greater than 130 knots.

(2) TO RAISE FLOATS.

(a) Turn float switch on engineer's instrument panel to "FLOATS UP."

b. EMERGENCY OPERATION.
(See figure 44.)

(1) TO LOWER FLOATS.

(a) Remove hand crank from stowage on starboard side of bulkhead below engineer's seat.

(b) Engage crank in socket marked "FAST," in center of bulkhead below engineer's seat, and crank counterclockwise.

(2) TO RAISE FLOATS.

(a) Insert crank in socket marked "FAST" and turn clockwise until load gets too heavy to operate easily. To raise floats remainder of the distance, move crank to "SLOW" socket, and continue to turn clockwise until floats are latched in up position.

5. AUXILIARY POWER PLANT OPERATION.
(See figure 7.)

To start the auxiliary power plant, first disconnect the auxiliary generator from either of the two buses at the main power distribution panel. (Turn selector switch to "OFF" position.) Set choke lever on "CHOKE" position. Wind rope around starting pulley and give a quick pull. Several attempts may be necessary to start in cold weather. Do not leave choke lever in "CHOKE" position after two pulls, except in very cold weather. Do not put load on generator until engine runs smoothly with choke lever set to "RUN."

To stop the unit, shut off fuel supply at selector valve on engineer's panel. An emergency stop may be made by pushing magneto ground button on magneto.

6. CENTRAL HEATER SYSTEM OPERATION.

The airplane central heater system consists of a burner, located under the navigator's table, which burns a mixture of gasoline vapor and air, and ducts to distribute heated air to outlets in the various compartments in the airplane. The burner unit is supplied with fuel from the main fuel tanks of the airplane through the same fuel valve which controls fuel flow to the auxiliary power unit and the tail anti-icer.

During flight, air pressure for the forced draft combustion chamber, as well as the hot air distribution ducts is furnished by a ram air scoop on the port side of the hull, under the wing. When ram air pressure is not available, air pressure is furnished by an electrically driven blower within the heater unit. The blower is automatically controlled by an air pressure switch, so that when the ram air pressure falls below a minimum value, the electric blower will keep the pressure up to the required operating value. An electrically driven fuel pump, supplies fuel to the combustion chamber. An automatic cut-out switch stops the fuel pump, if the fire in the combustion chamber goes out accidentally.

a. TO START THE CENTRAL HEATER.

(1) First be sure fuel supply valve on engineer's panel is turned on.

(2) Open intake air scoop on port side of hull in radio operator-navigator's compartment.

(3) Make sure that line switch on main power distribution panel is on proper bus (line switch is marked "PITOT HEATER" and "WINDSHIELD WIPER").

(4) Turn heater control switch to "START." This will energize igniter and fuel pump; also blower, if needed. After a few minutes, when glow unit of heater is hot enough to ignite fuel, turn control switch to "RUN." This will shut off the igniter, but will leave the blower and fuel pump circuits closed, and these circuits will then be controlled by the automatic cut-off switches.

CAUTION
If intake air scoops are closed temporarily for take-offs or landings, they must be opened again as soon as possible, if heater has been started.

b. TO STOP THE CENTRAL HEATER.—Turn the control switch off. Be sure to close air scoop before landing.

7. WING AND TAIL ANTI-ICER OPERATION.
(See figures 21 and 23.)

The wing anti-icing system is designed to prevent formation of ice on the surfaces, rather than to de-ice the surfaces after ice has started to form. It is therefore important to start operating the system BEFORE ICING CONDITIONS ARE ENCOUNTERED. Anti-icer temperature gages are to the left of the flight engineer's seat. Automatic thermostatic controls dump hot air from ducts when temperature rises to 150°C (302°F).

Operation of the wing anti-icer is accomplished as follows:

a. Turn "MAIN BATTERY" switch on at main power distribution panel.

b. Turn "ANTI-ICERS AND HEATER" switch on at main distribution panel.

c. Place "WING ANTI-ICER" switch in "OPEN" position on pilot's switch panel. If temperature rises above 150°C (302°F) the automatic control has failed.

The switch should then be operated manually "on" and "off" to keep temperatures below 150° C. (302° F).

d. Place "WING ANTI-ICER" switch in "CLOSED" position to shut off hot air supply.

The tail anti-icing system like the wing anti-icing system, should be turned on BEFORE ICING CONDITIONS ARE ENCOUNTERED.

Controls for the tail anti-icer consist of a fuel shut-off valve, located at the right of the flight engineer, and a switch and damper control, located on the forward face of bulkhead 7.

CAUTION

In the event the hot air ducts fail to operate on one side during icing conditions, the WING ANTI-ICER switch should be closed. Failure to do so would result in the formation of ice on one side only causing critical flight characteristics.

Operation of the tail anti-icer is accomplished as follows:

a. Turn "MAIN BATTERY" switch on at main distribution panel.

b. Place "TAIL ANTI-ICER" switch on proper bus.

c. Open fuel valve in flight engineer's compartment.

d. Turn anti-icer switch on at bulkhead 7.

e. Pull damper control lock down and pull damper control fully out, 30 seconds after turning on switch at bulkhead 7.

To shut off heater:

a. Close fuel valve in flight engineer's compartment.

b. Turn off anti-icer switch at bulkhead 7.

c. Move air scoop control to "CLOSED" position.

d. Turn off switch at main distribution panel.

CAUTION

Damper must be closed during take-offs and landings. It must be fully opened during operation of heater.

8. PROPELLER ANTI-ICER OPERATION.

The anti-icer control for propeller anti-icing fluid is a rheostat, located on the pilot's switch panel. Operation of the propeller anti-icer is accomplished as follows:

a. Turn on fluid supply valve. This valve is located below reservoir on the aft face of bulkhead 4, port side.

b. Turn "MAIN BATTERY" switch on at main distribution panel.

c. Turn "ANTI-ICERS AND HEATERS" switch on at main distribution panel.

d. Turn "ANTI-ICER" control to desired rate of flow.

9. OPERATION OF MISCELLANEOUS EQUIPMENT.

a. COMPARTMENT VENTILATORS.—Ventilators are located in the ceiling of the radio operator-navigator's compartment and the engineer's compartment, on each side of the ship. The ventilators are water-sealed with gaskets and held closed with spring and toggle latches. The ventilators must be closed for landings and take-offs. Ventilators in the engineer's compartment must be open when the auxiliary power unit is running, except during landings and take-offs.

b. BILGE PUMP.—A bilge pump is attached to the auxiliary power unit and is driven by the unit engine. To engage the pump, push down on lever at back of engine. Speed of engine and pump may be increased by removing load from auxiliary generator with switch on main power distribution panel. Bilge pump hose is stowed on aft face of bulkhead 5, port side.

c. ANCHOR.

(1) TO CAST ANCHOR.

(See figure 28.)

(a) Fit float gear hand crank into anchor reel socket on port side of bomber's compartment. Station one man here to operate crank.

(b) Detail second man, equipped with safety belt, to outside of ship to perform following operations:

(c) Open door of anchor box at latch in up position with webbing strap and dot fastener provided.

(d) Hook safety belt in forward snap, facing aft.

(e) Take out anchor. Set it upside down on walk rail in handhole slot.

(f) Unfold anchor while in upside-down position.

(g) Place anchor cable in guide eye in walk rail.

(h) Drop anchor overboard. (Man inside must release ratchet of reel.)

(i) When anchor hits bottom, release pendant from stowage and secure clamp to anchor cable. Throw pendant overboard and slack off anchor cable until pendant cable is taking pull of the anchor line.

(j) Man inside must secure anchor reel with latch.

(2) TO WEIGH ANCHOR.

(a) Break out anchor by overrunning with engines. Be sure to maneuver in such a way as to keep tension on pendant, being careful not to allow tension to be taken by anchor line or reel.

(b) When anchor is free, reel in anchor line until pendant clamp can be removed. Stow pendant, clamp and lizard with strap provided in anchor box.

(c) Reel in anchor until top of anchor is level with the water.

(d) Use safety belt in same position as before.

(e) Reach below walk rail and disengage cable from guide eye.

(f) Set anchor in upside down position on walk rail.

(g) Unlock and fold anchor.

(h) Stow anchor in anchor box with cable end of shank pointing forward.

(i) Close and latch door of anchor box.

10. MOVEMENT OF FLIGHT PERSONNEL.

Unrestricted movement of flight personnel from one end of the ship to the other is made possible by the central passageway. The watertight bulkhead doors should be left open, except in an emergency.

Escape from the airplane during flight may be made through the waist gun blisters or the tunnel gun hatch.

When the airplane is on land or water, the hatches in the top of the bow turret and the pilot's compartment are available as additional escape hatches.

In operating the airplane, the pilot and flight engineer coordinate their activities through the interphone, or by means of the signal light system previously described. The radio operator is responsible for checking the line switches and generator and battery bus switches on the main power distribution panel aft of his table.

The crew positions at battle stations are as follows:
One man at pilot's station.
One man at engineer's station.
One man at bomber-bow gunner's station.
One man at radio operator's station.
Two men at waist gun stations.
One man at tunnel gun station.
One man at radar operator's station.

1. APU Generator
2. APU Oil Tank
3. APU Fuel Line
4. APU DC Voltage Regulator
5. D-C Feed
6. A-C Feed
7. APU Engine
8. Propeller Anti-icing Fluid Pump

Figure 7—Auxiliary Power Unit

Figure 8 below illustrates the arrangement of the various operating compartments and the watertight bulkheads which separate them.

Location of emergency equipment and exits is illustrated in Figure 45 in Section IV of this handbook.

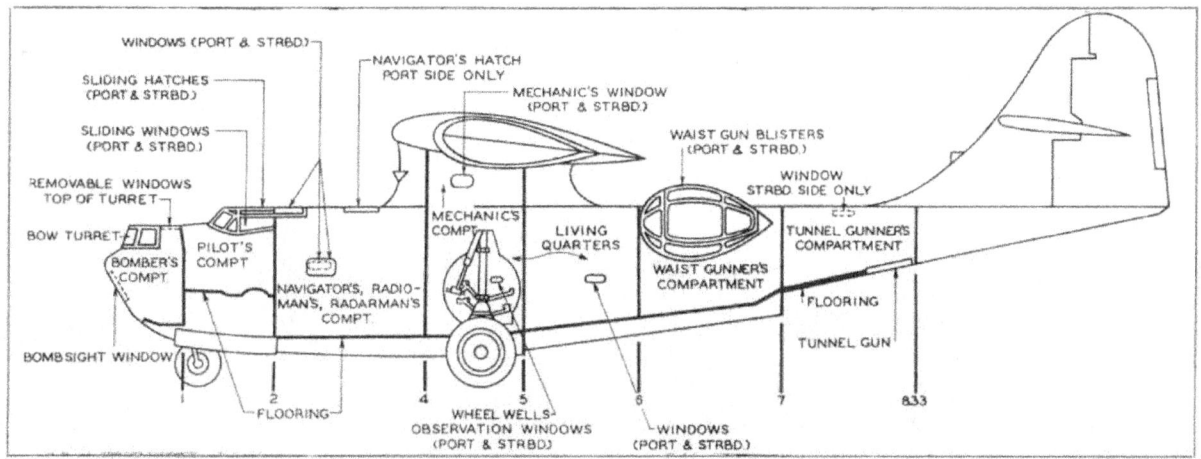

Figure 8—Compartments, Windows and Flooring

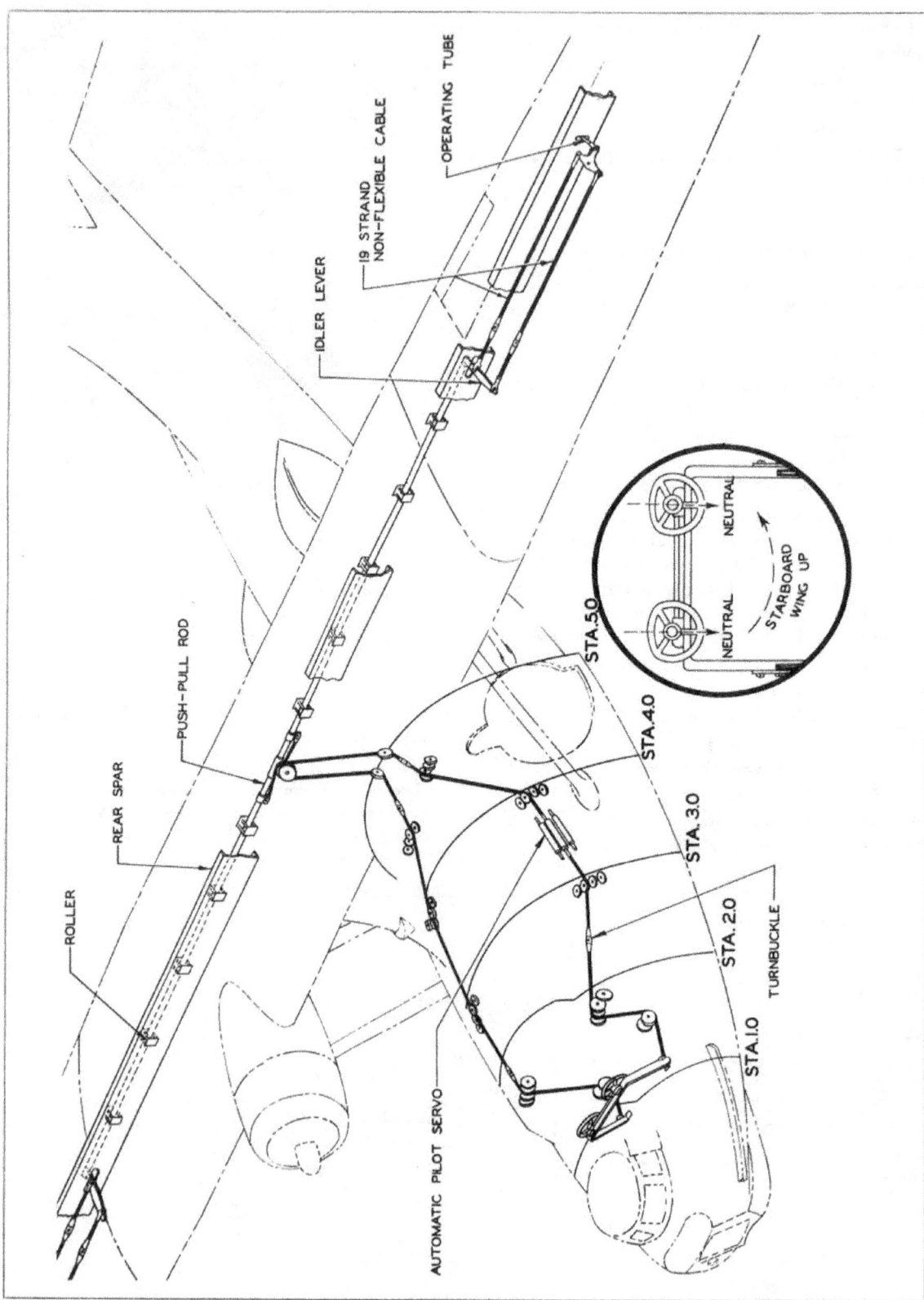

Figure 9—Aileron Controls Diagram

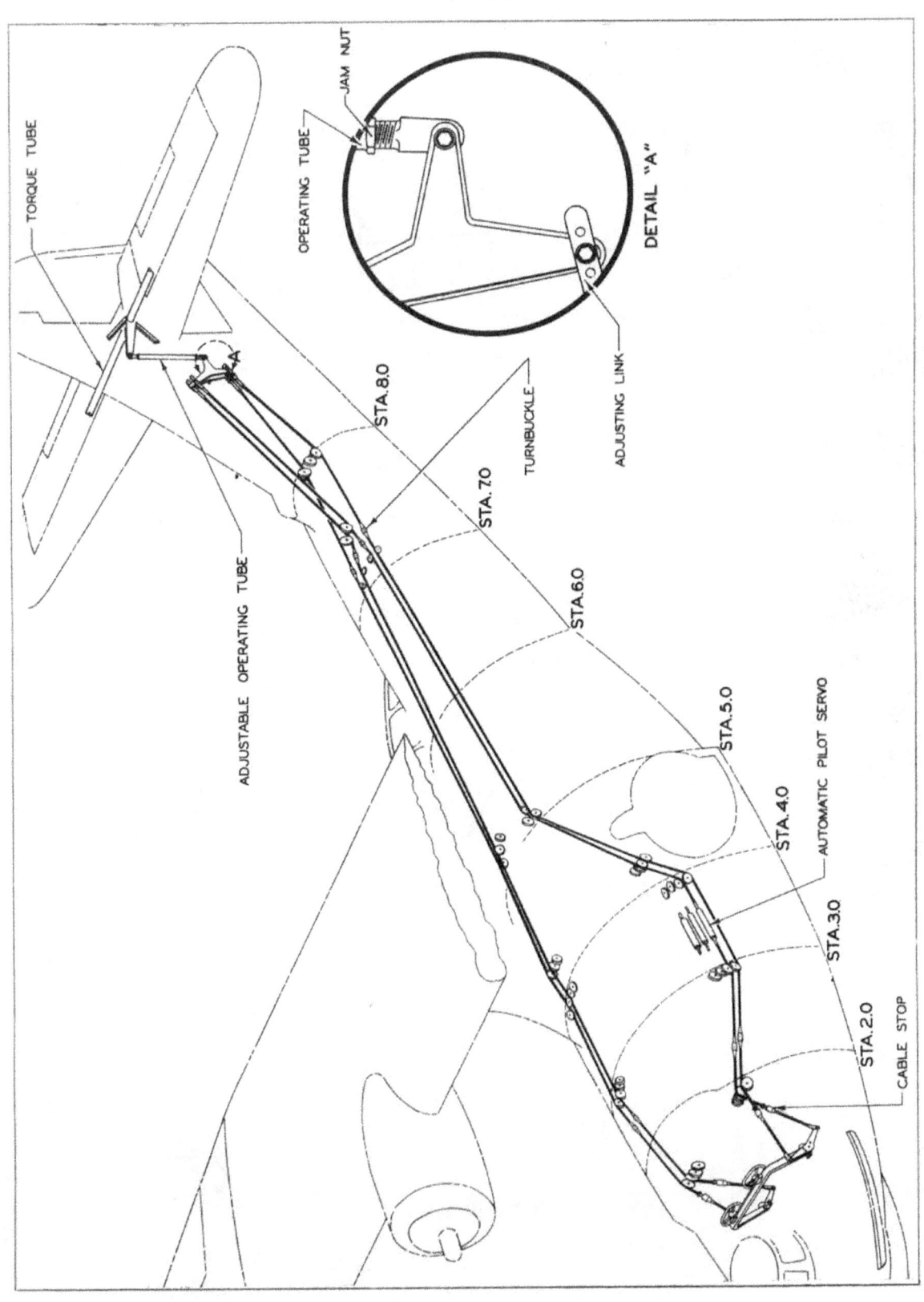

Figure 10—Elevator Controls Diagram

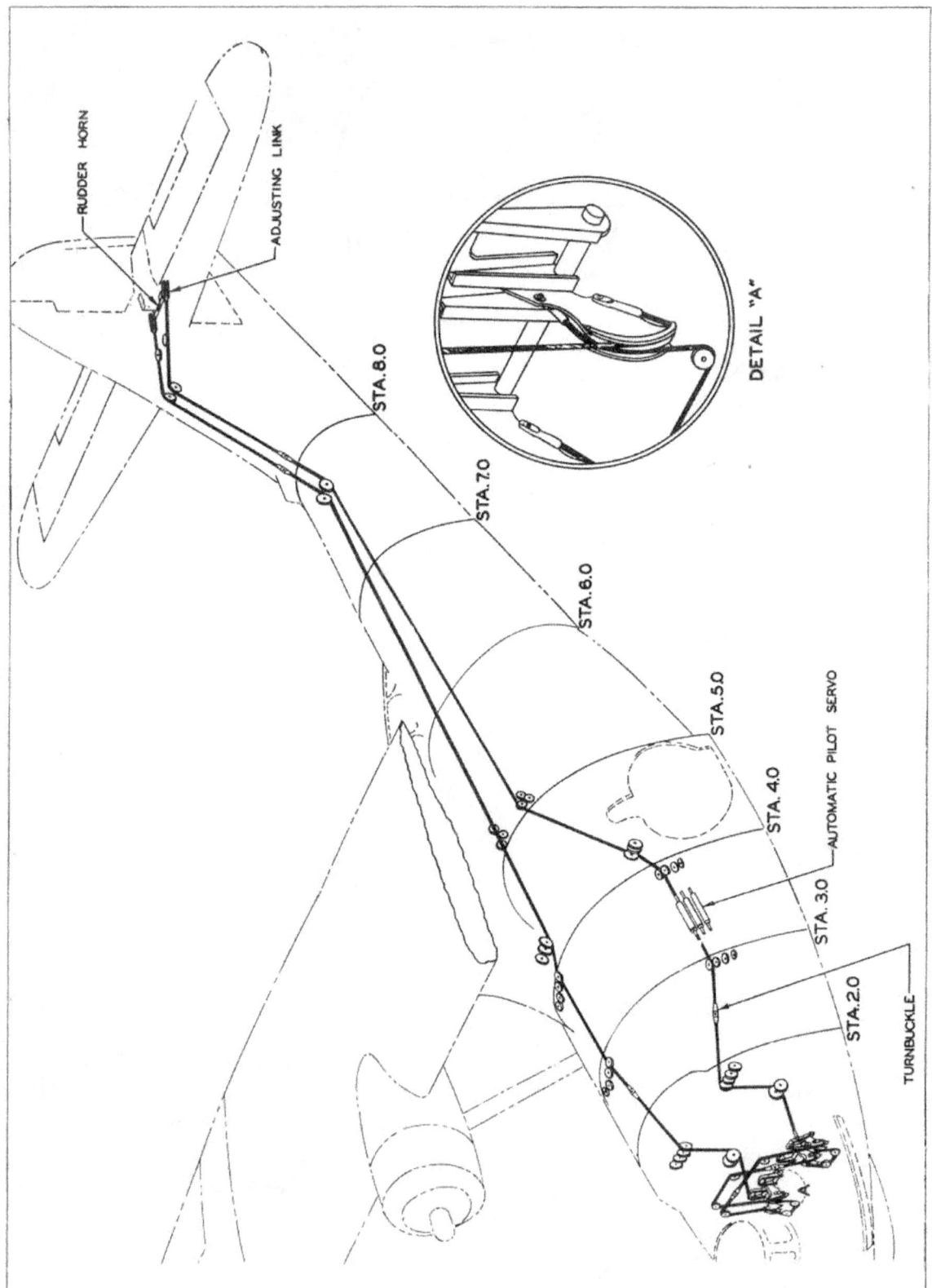

Figure 11 – Rudder Controls Diagram

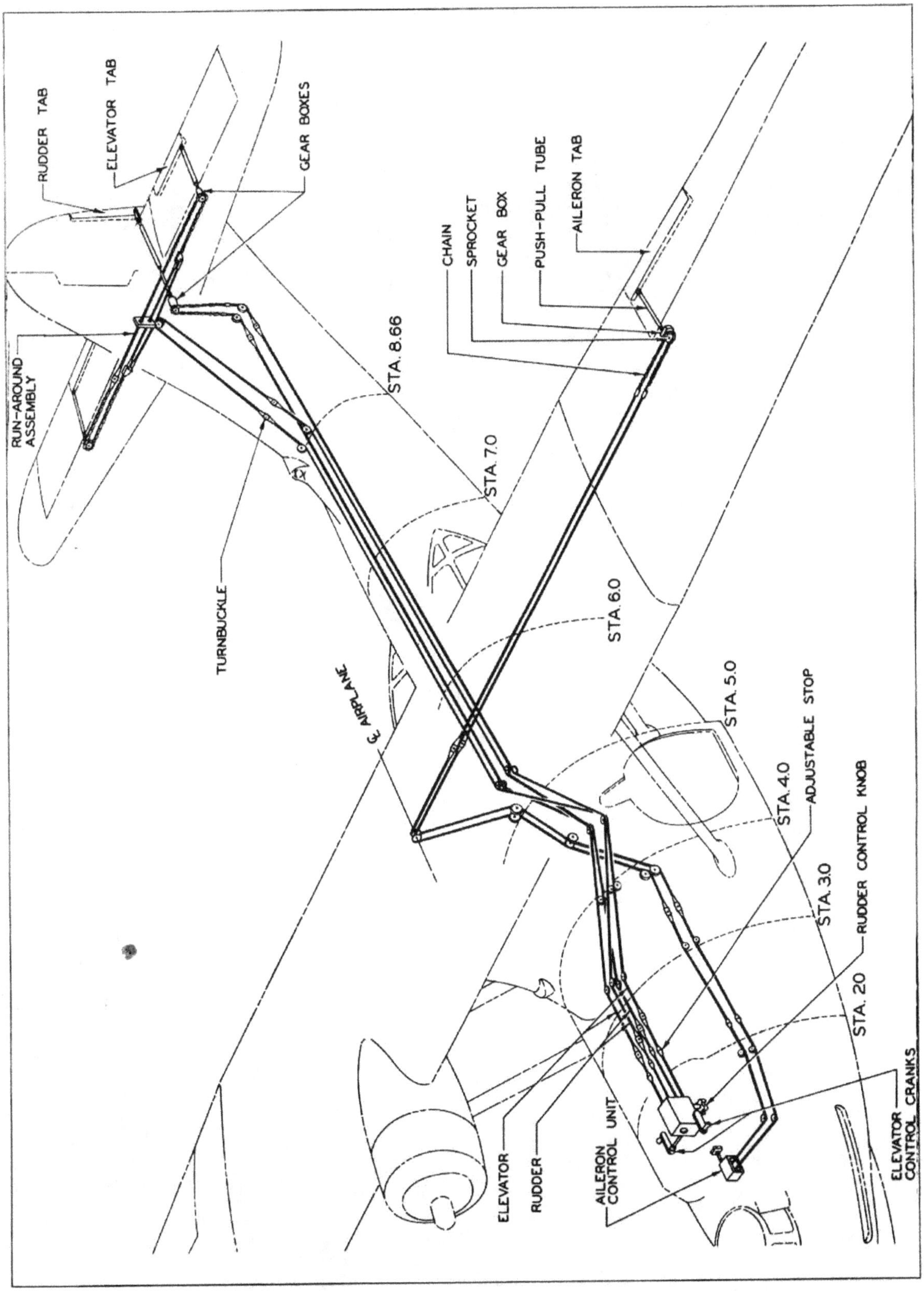

Figure 12 – Tab Controls Diagram

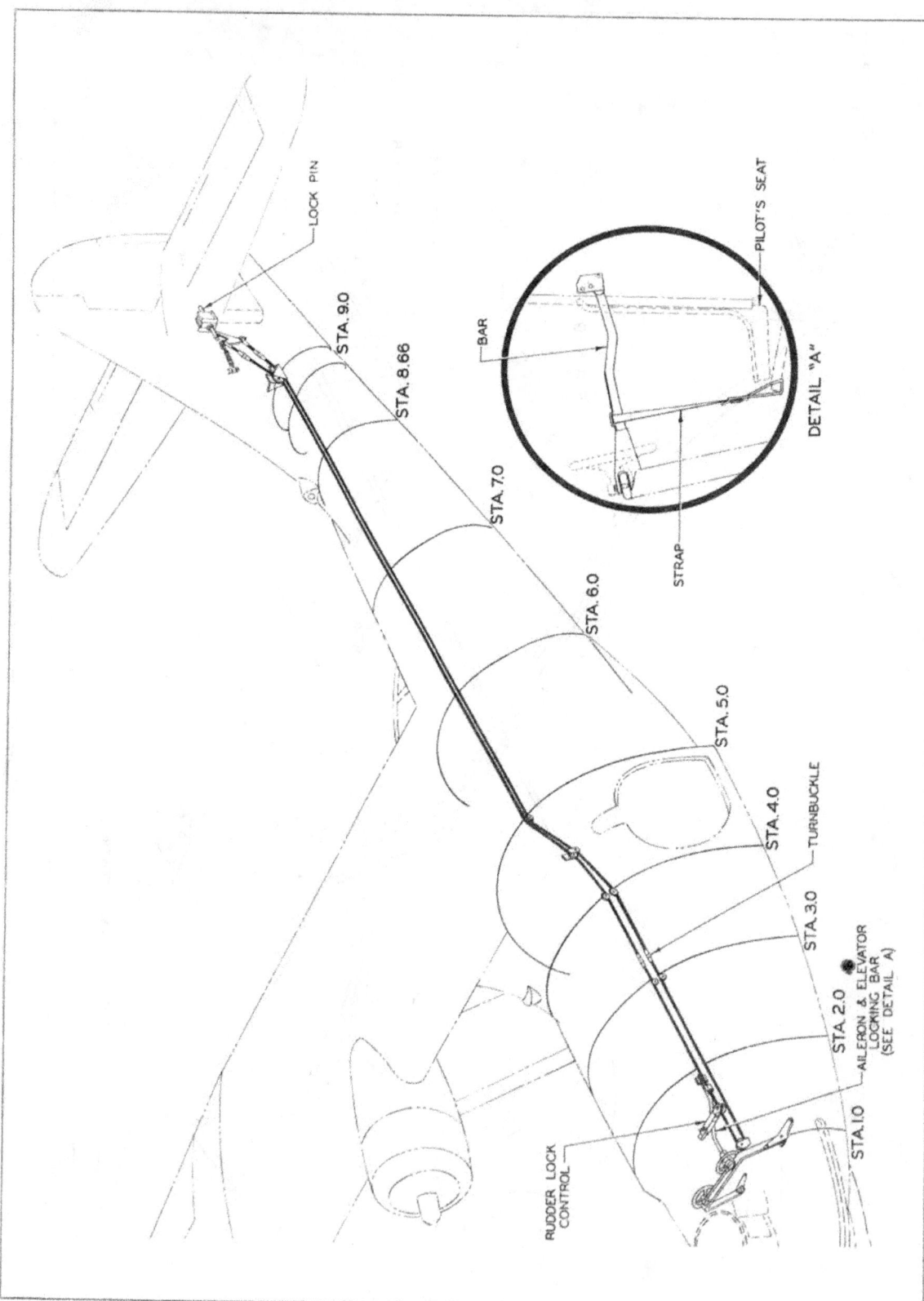

Figure 13—Controls Lock Diagram

Section I

AN 01-5MA-1

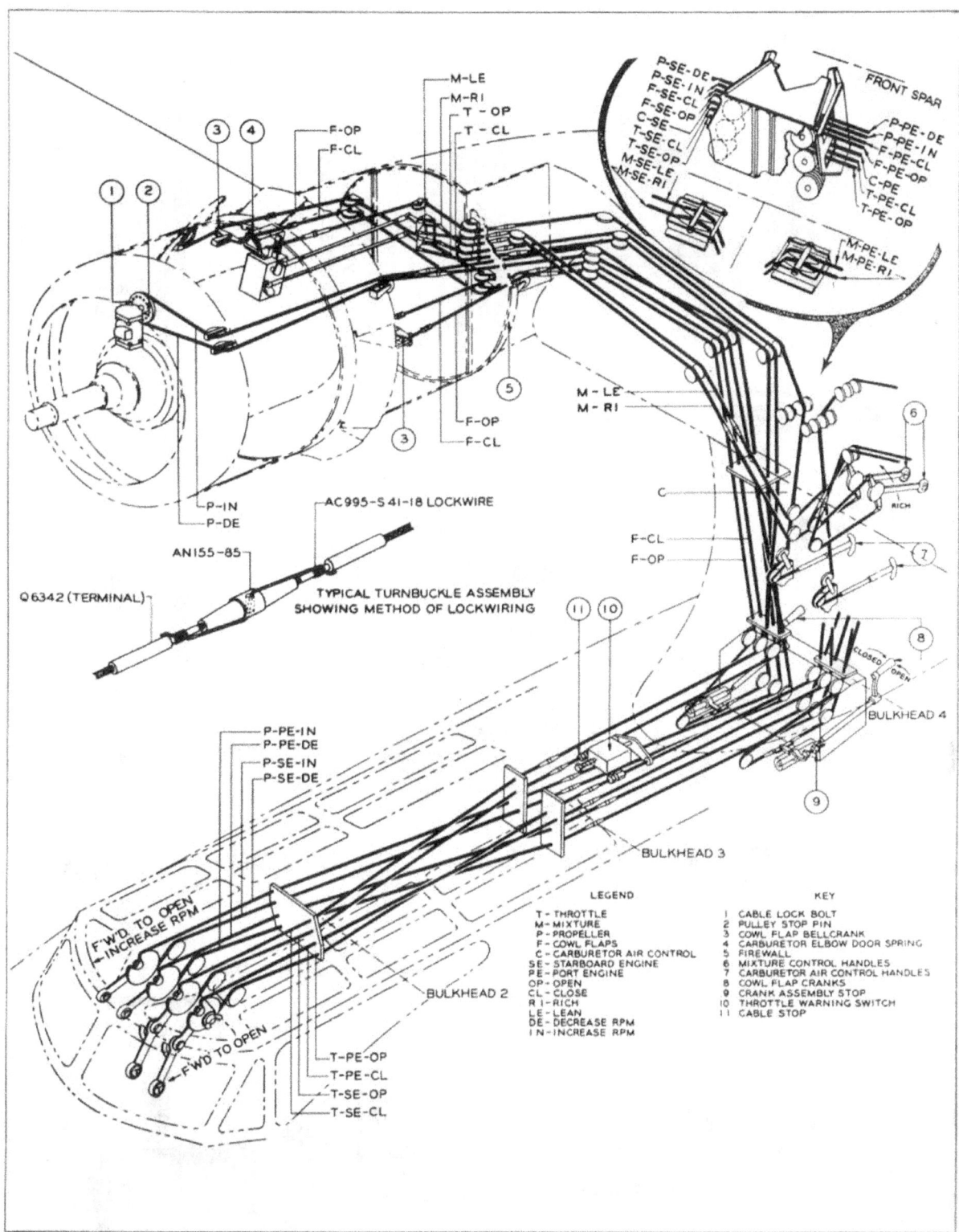

Figure 14—Engine Controls Diagram

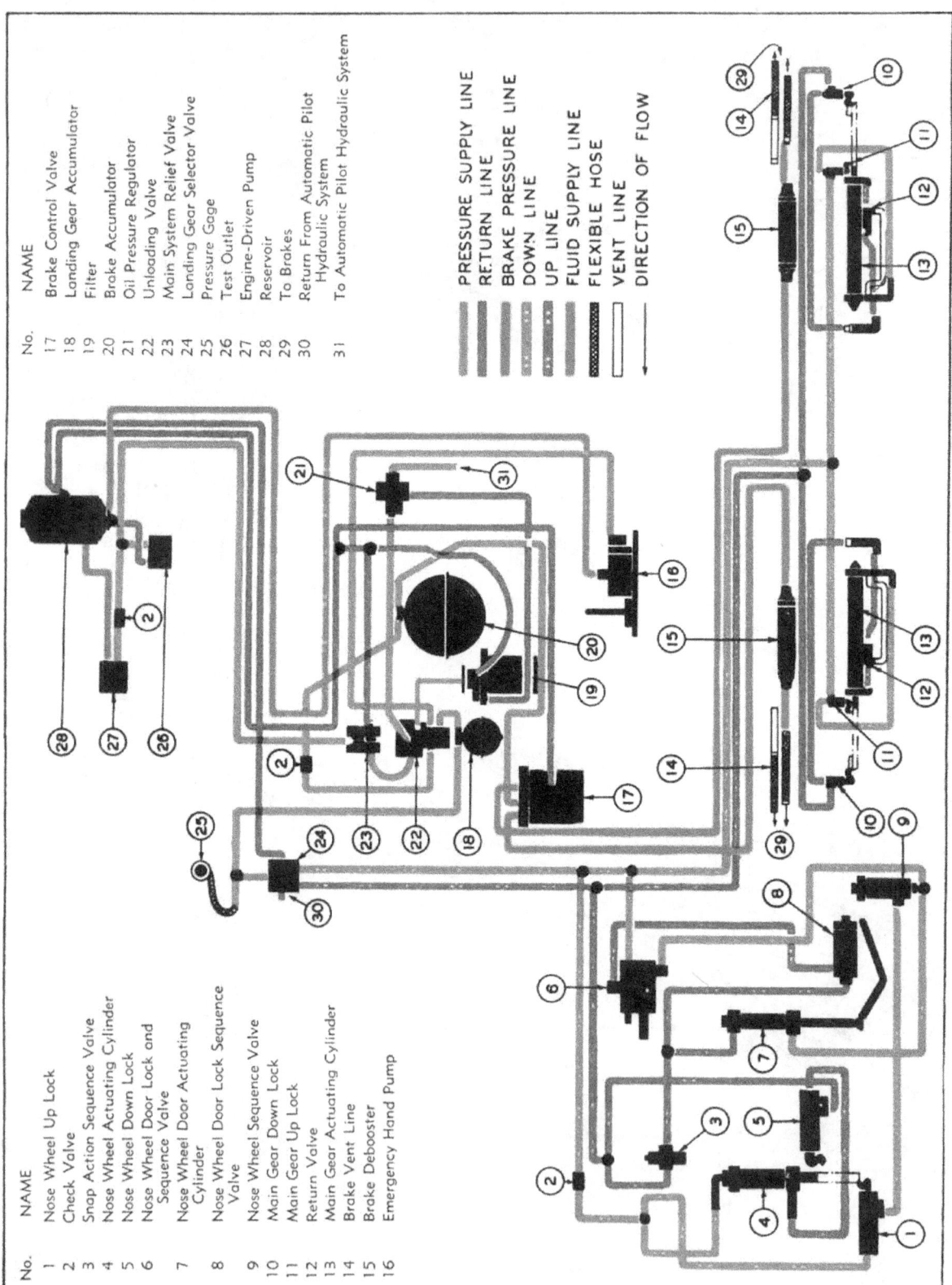

Figure 15—Main Hydraulic System Diagram

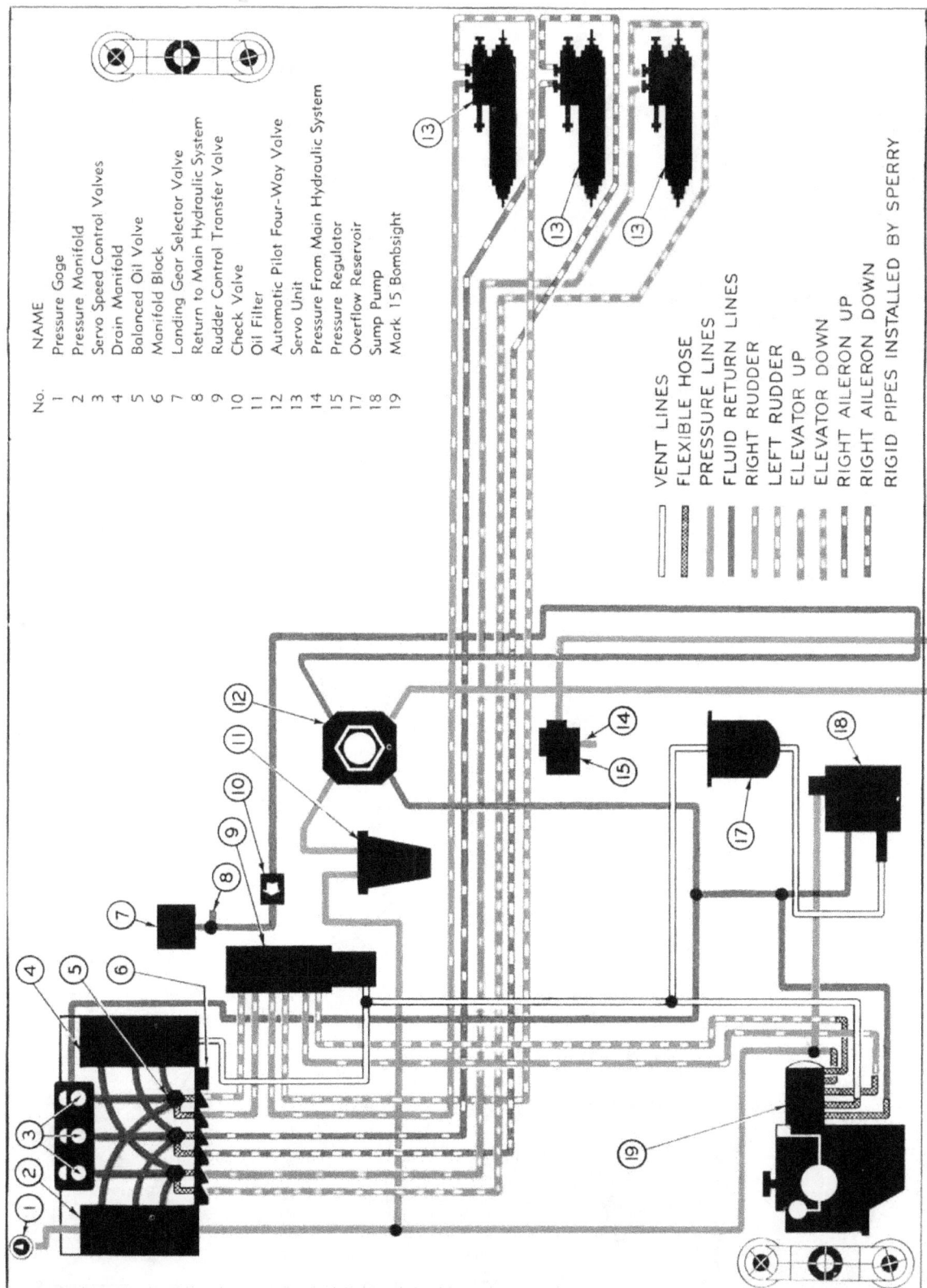

Figure 16—Gyropilot Hydraulic System

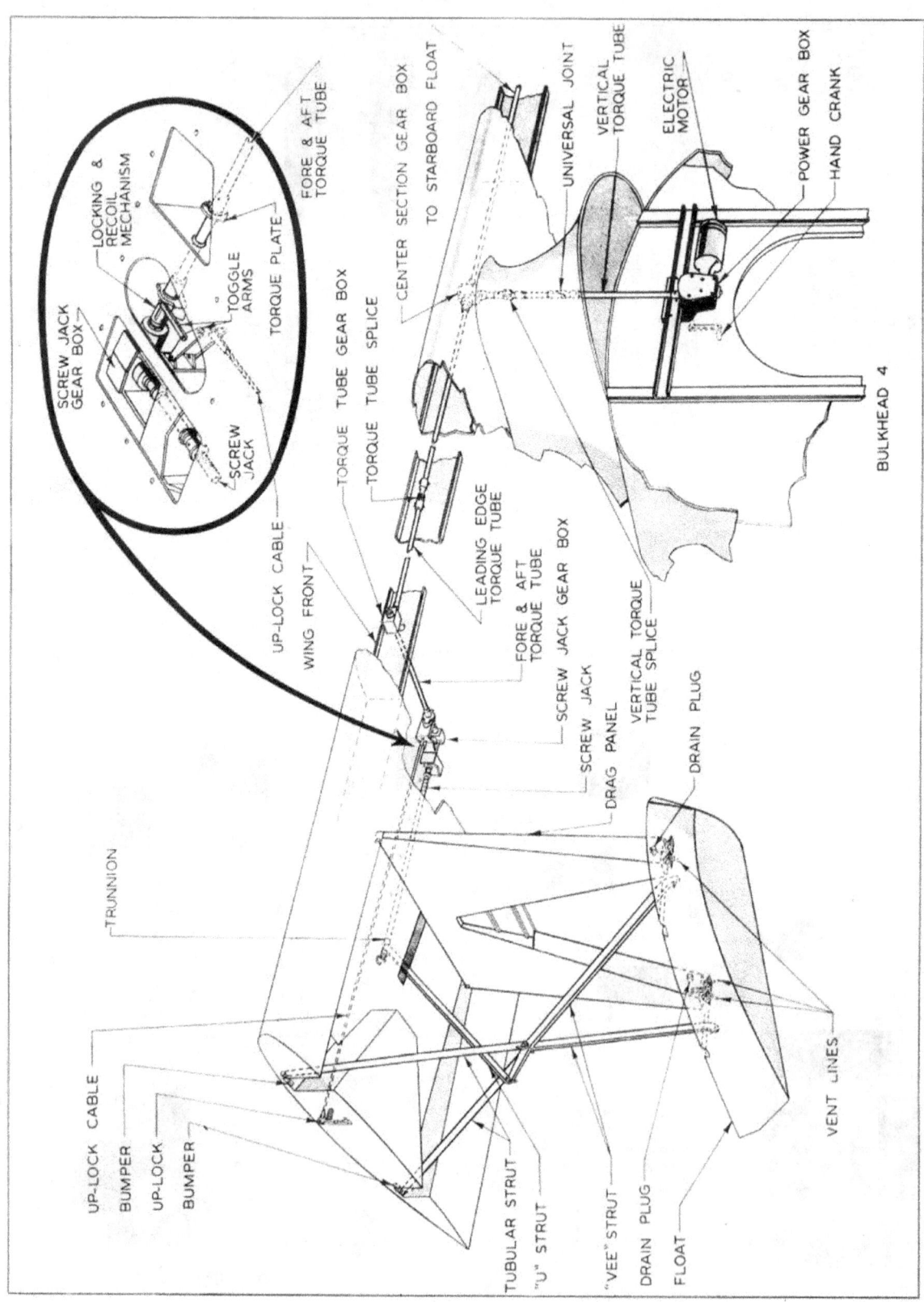

Figure 17—Float Retracting Mechanism

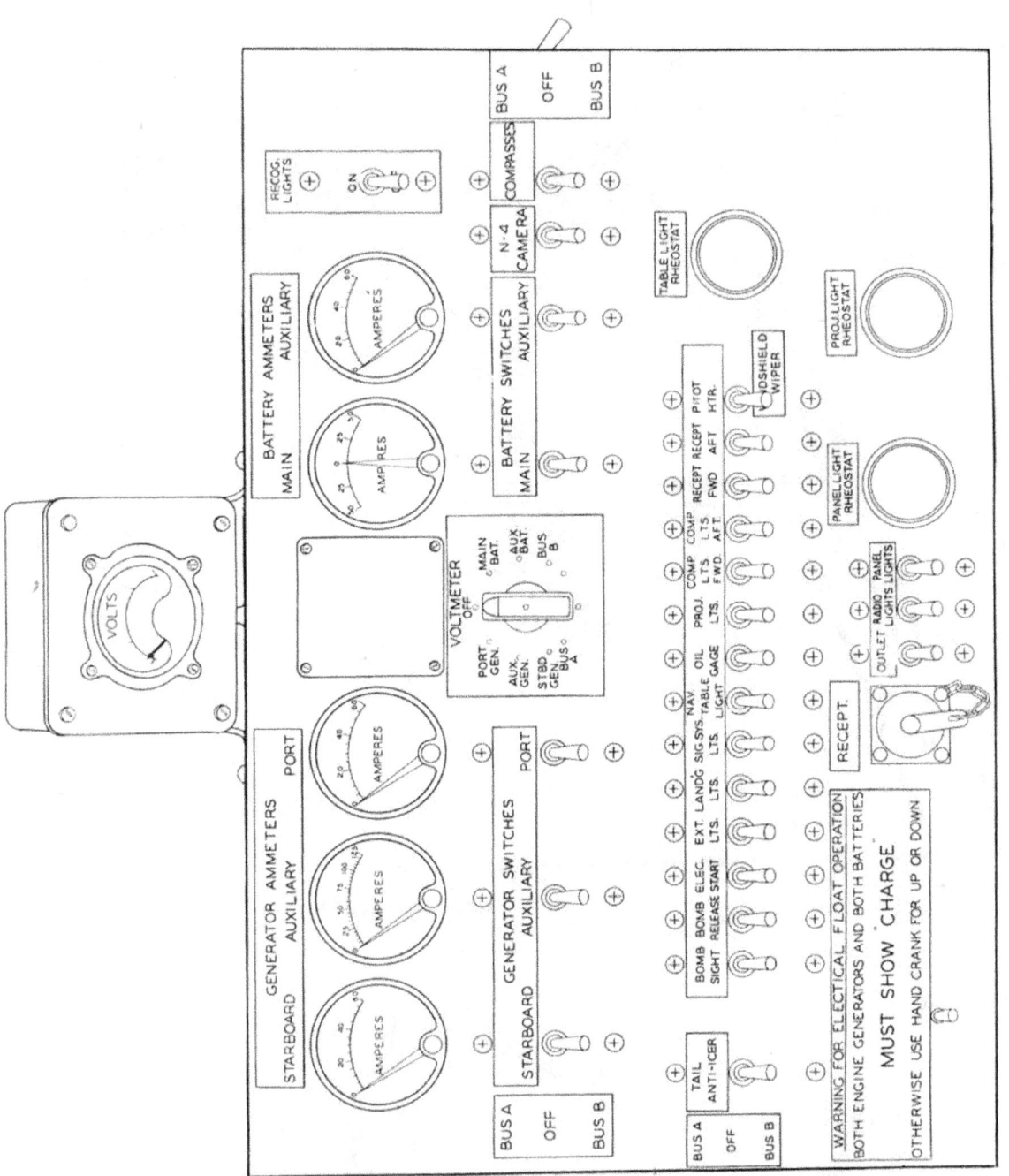

Figure 18—Main Power Distribution Panel

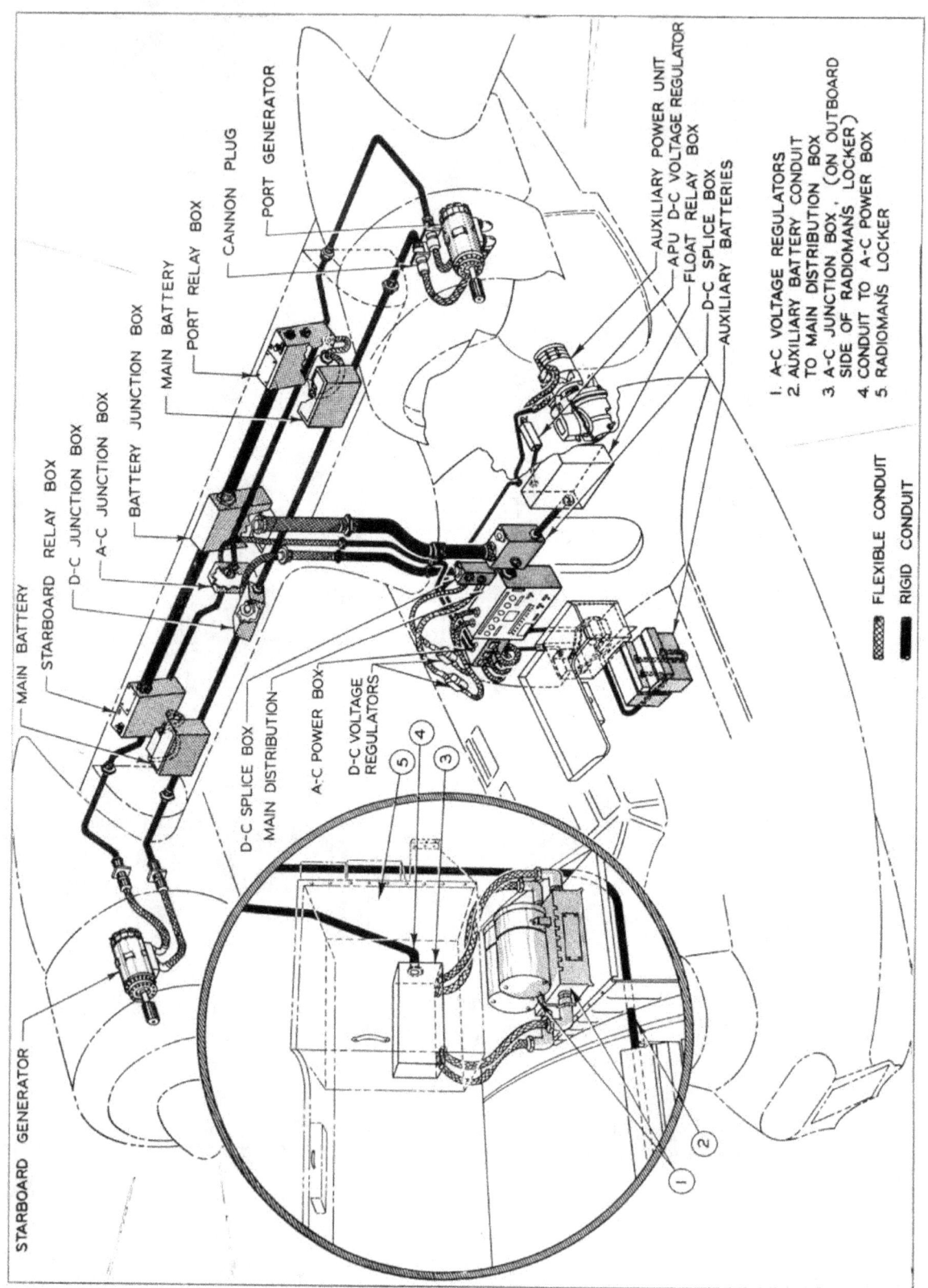

Figure 19—Power Distribution System

AN 01-5MA-1

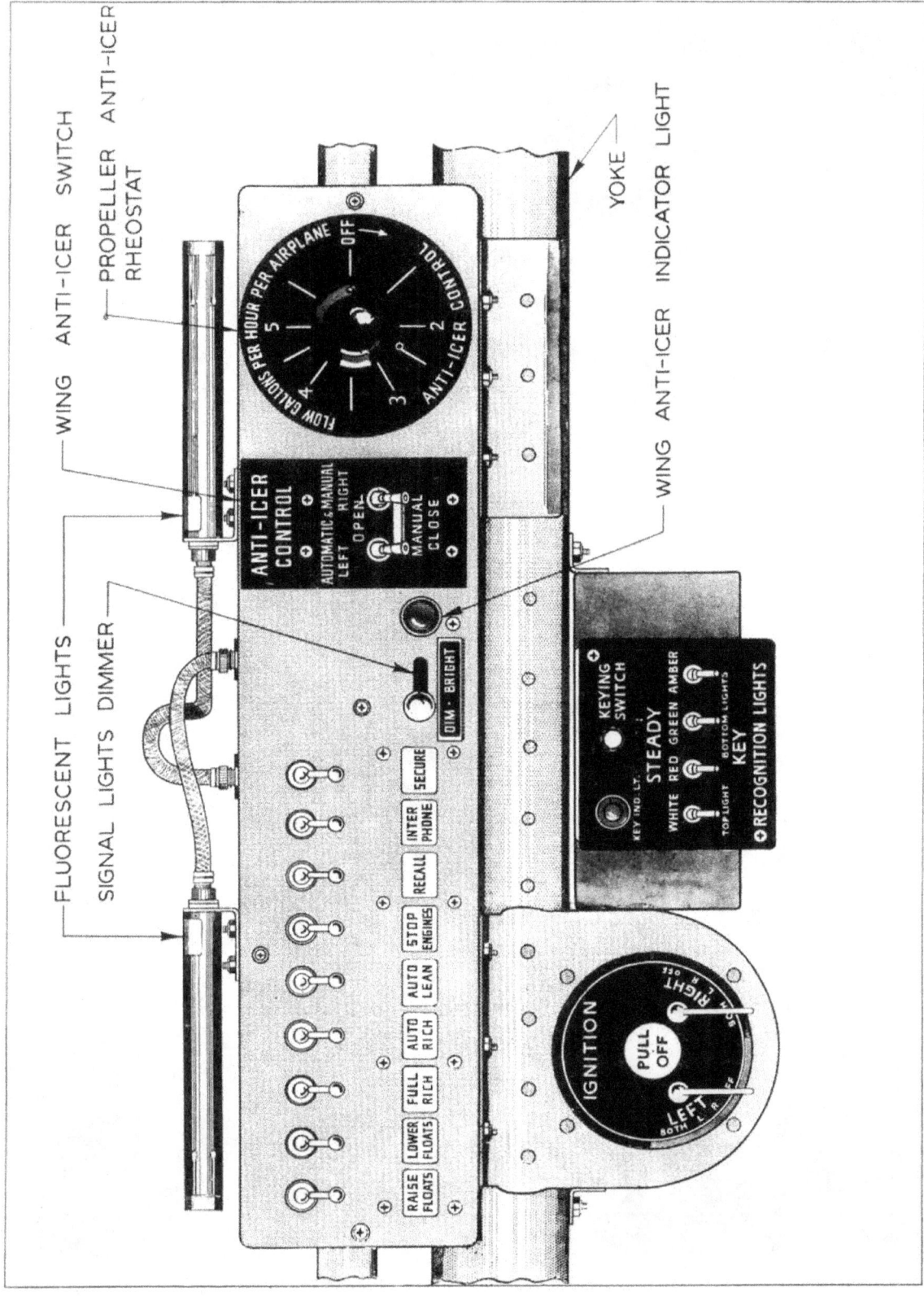

Figure 20—Electrical Equipment on Pilot's Yoke

Figure 21—Tail Anti-Icer Controls

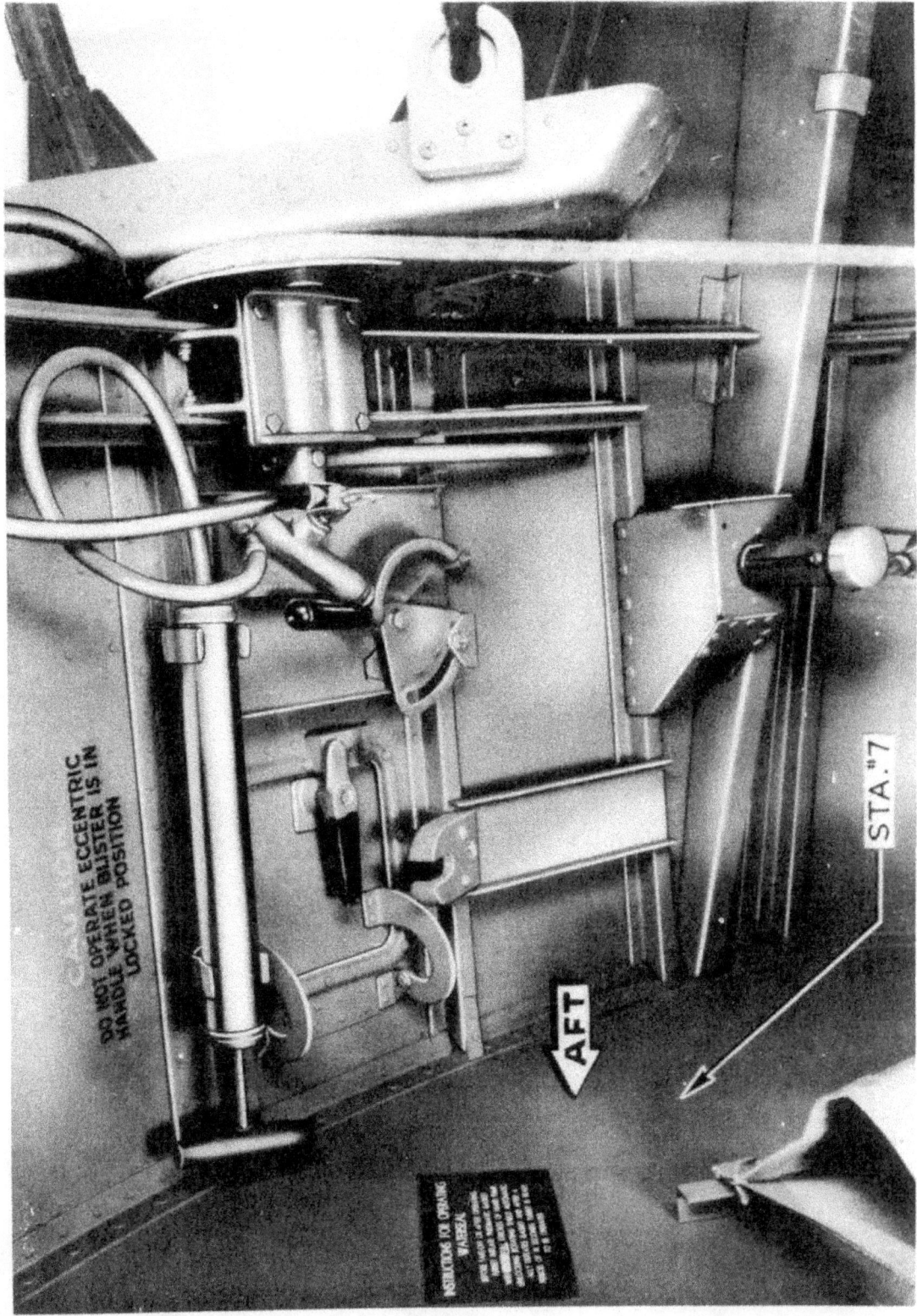

Figure 22—Waterseal Inflation Mechanism for Waist Gun Blister

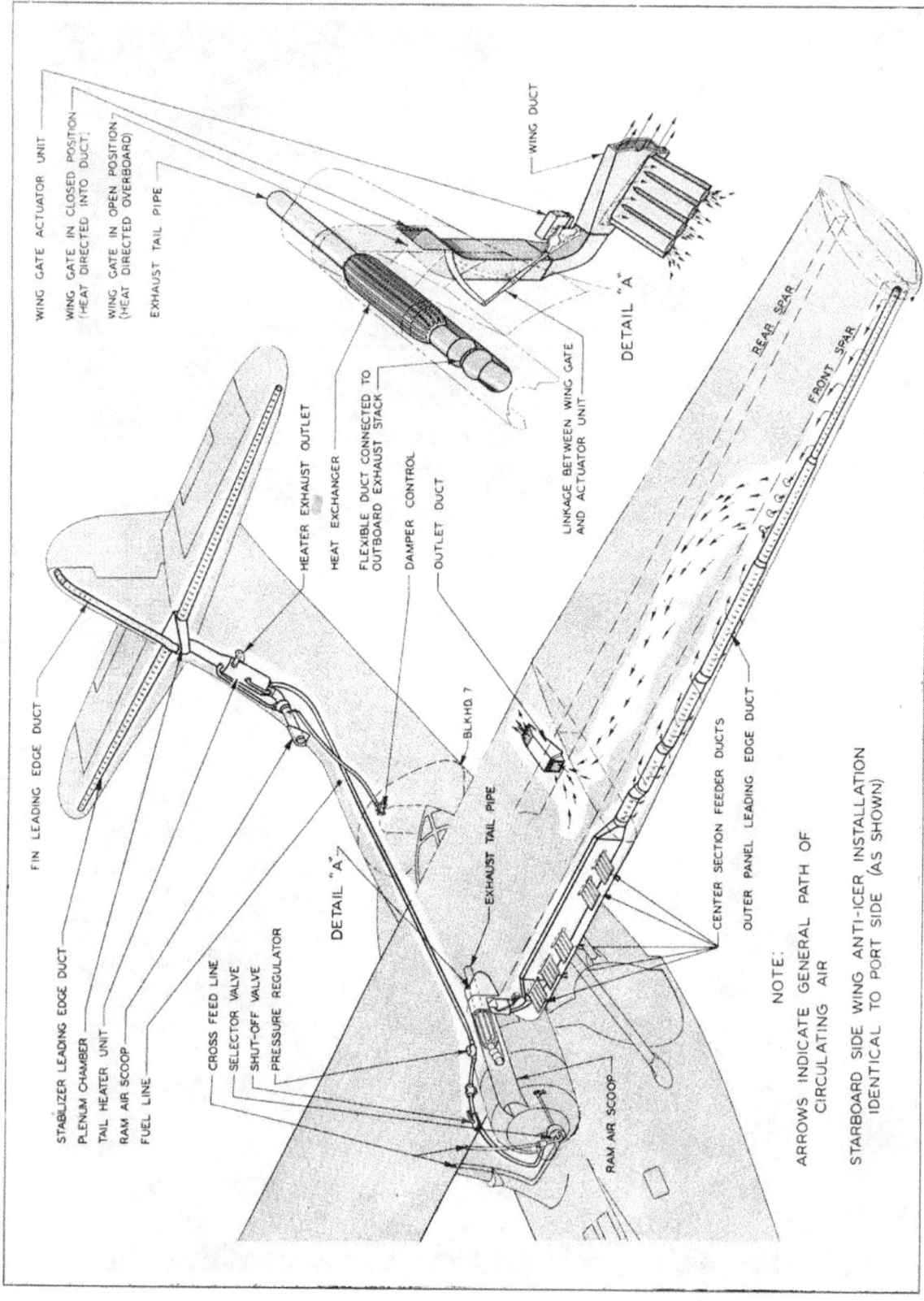

Figure 23—Heat Anti-Icing Systems

AN 01-5MA-1

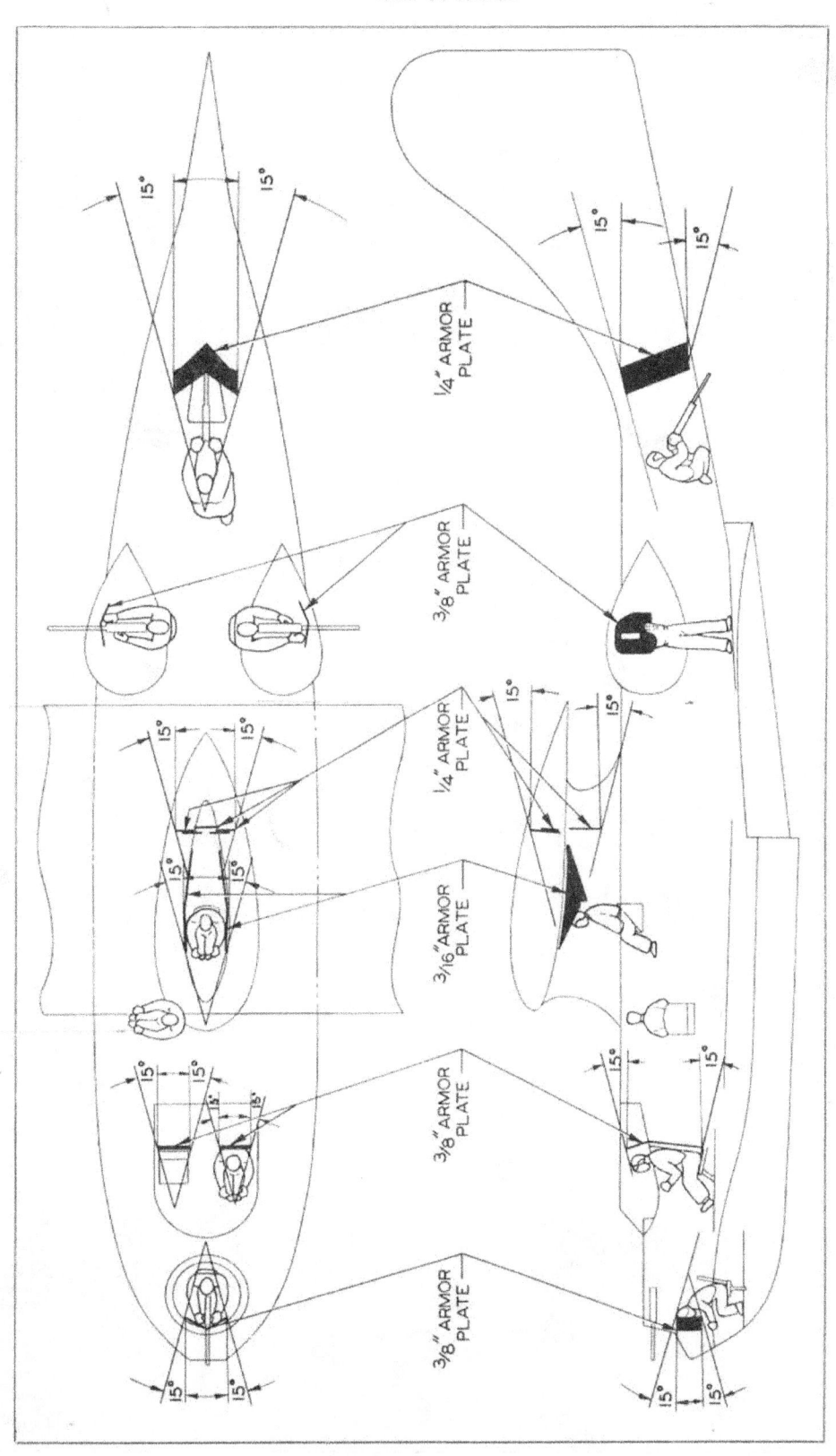

Figure 24—Angles of Armor Protection (Airplanes Prior to Bur. Ser. No. 46580)

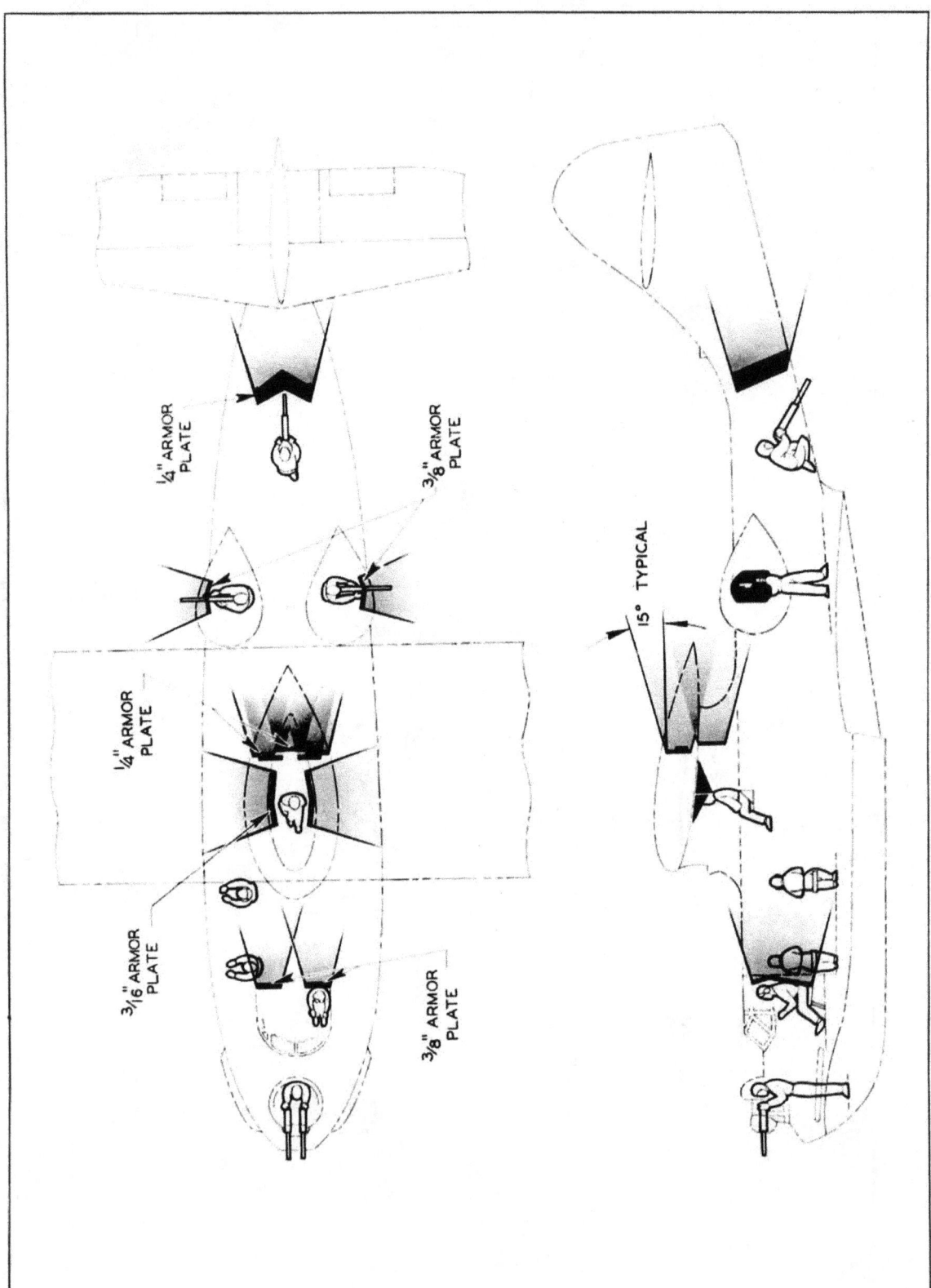

Figure 25—Angles of Armor Protection (Bureau Serial No. 46580 and on)

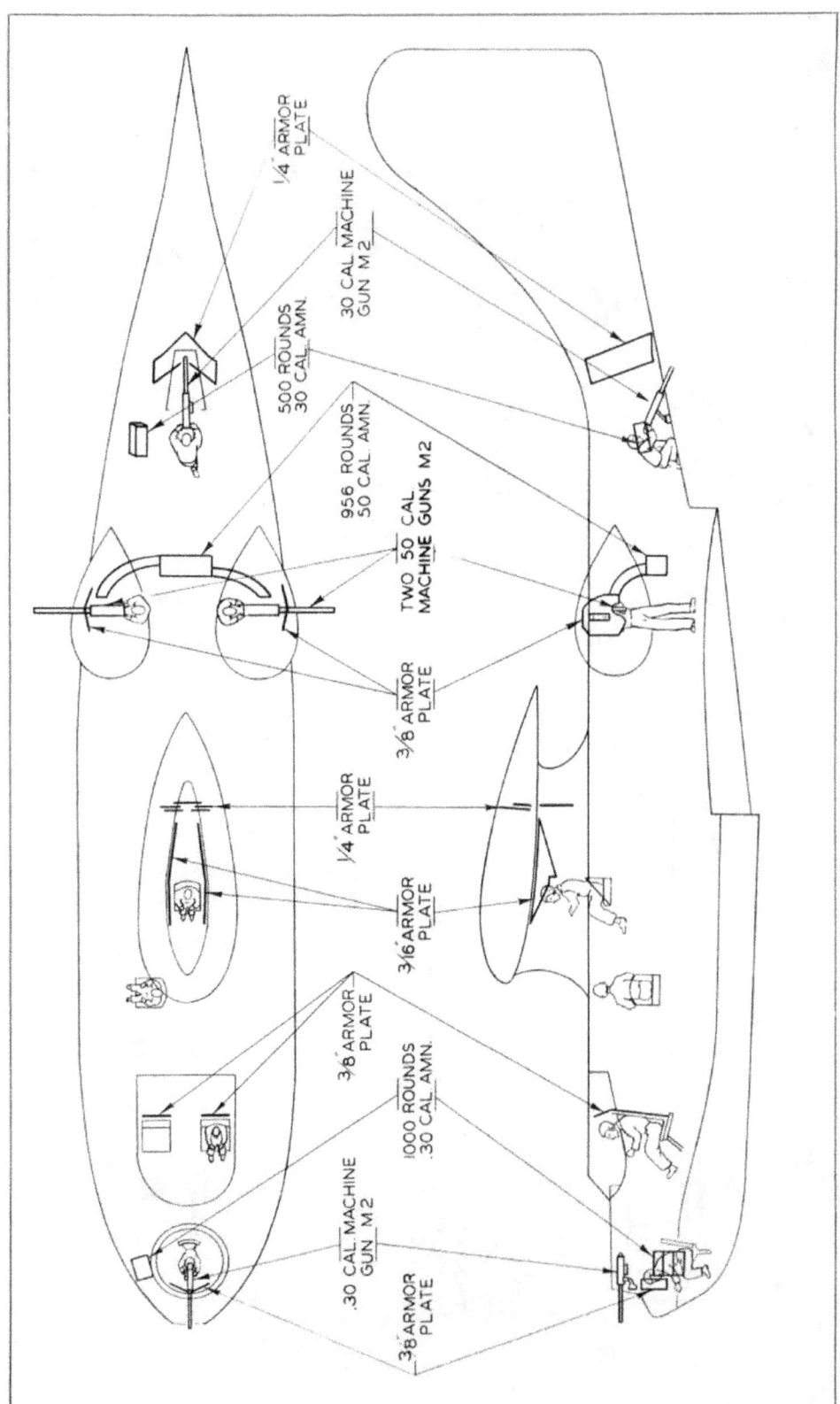

Figure 26—Defensive Armament Diagram (Airplanes prior to Bur. Ser. No. 46580)

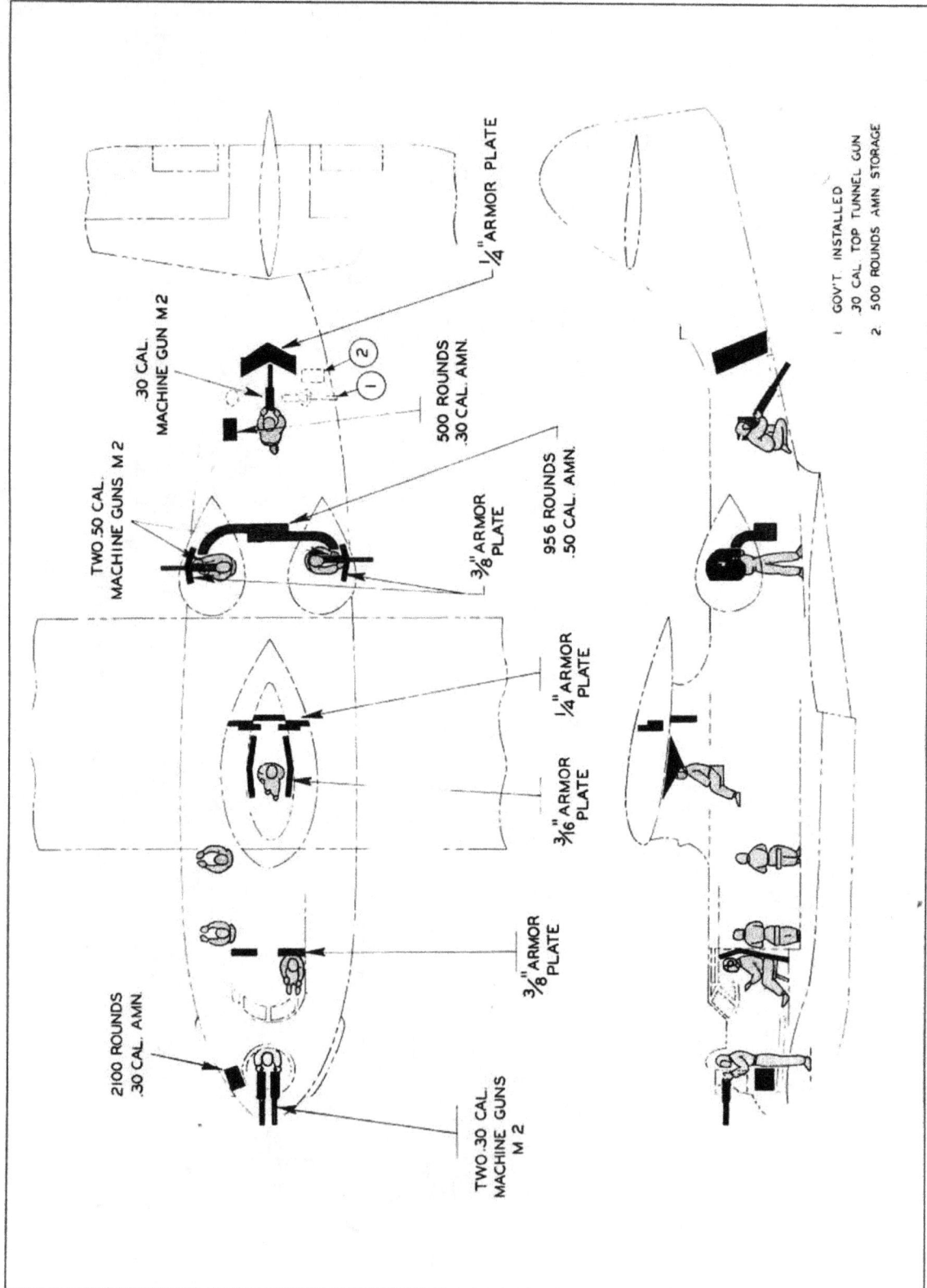

Figure 27 – Defensive Armament Diagram (Bureau Serial No. 46580 and on)

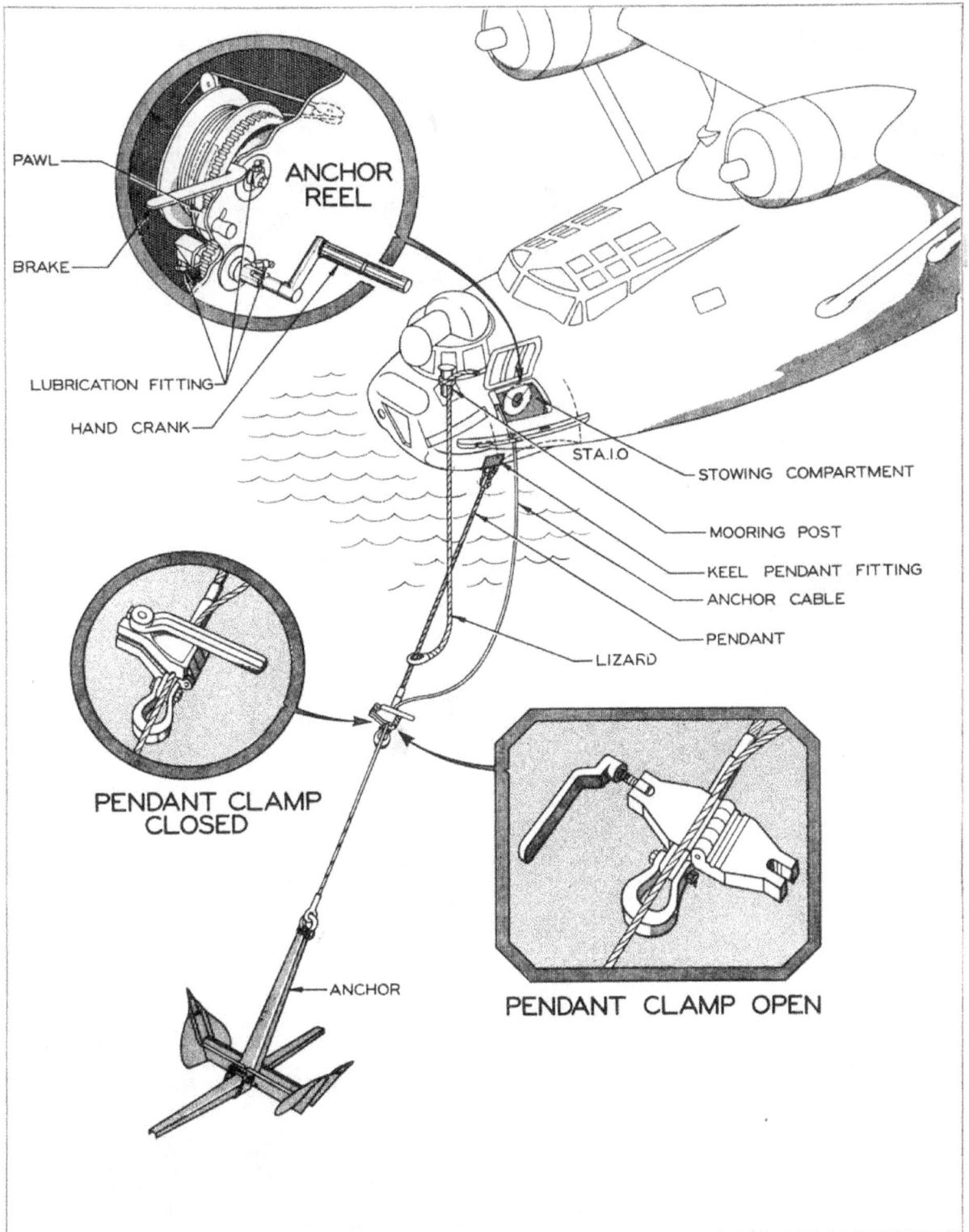

Figure 28—Anchor Gear Out

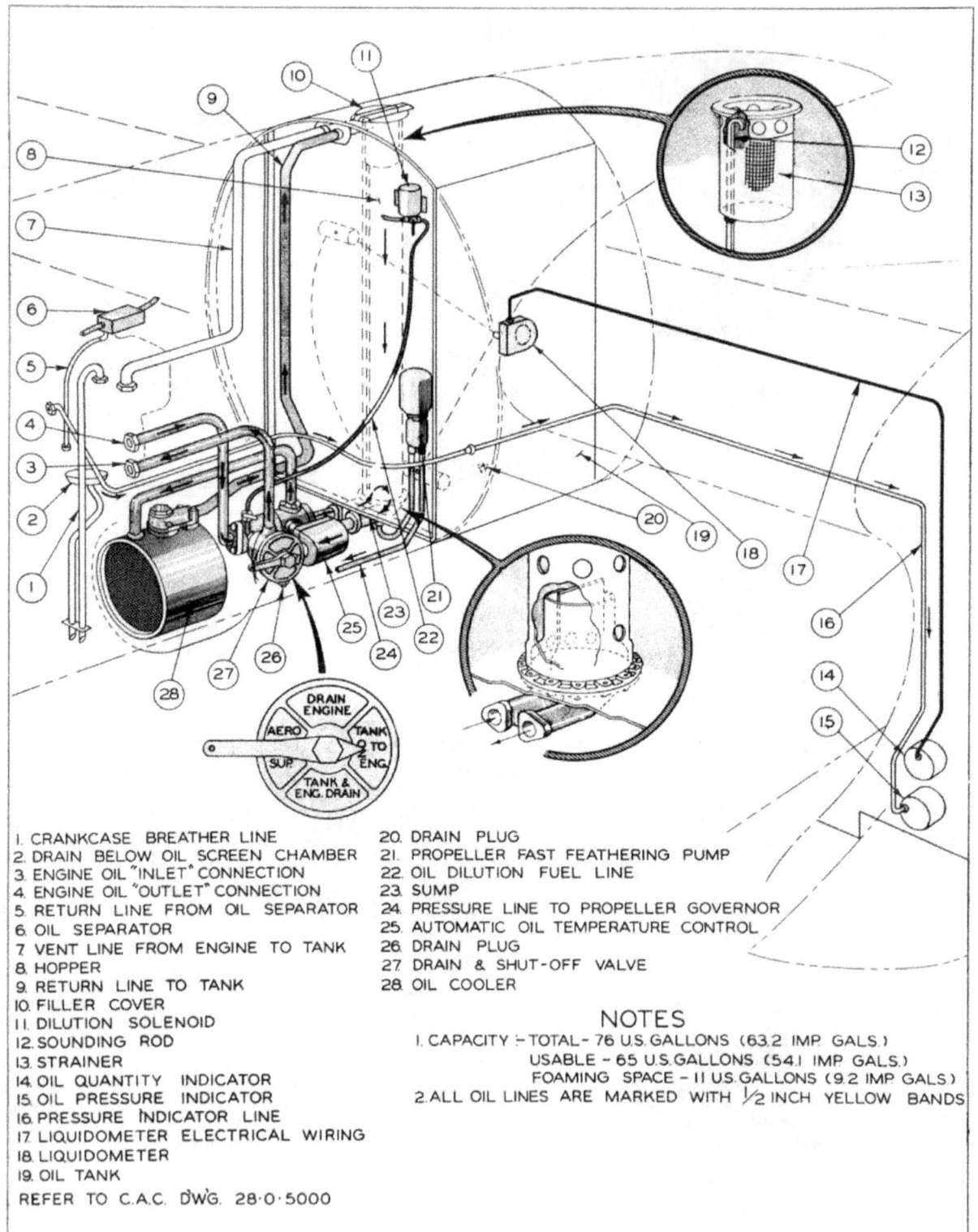

Figure 29—Oil System Diagram

SECTION II
PILOT OPERATING INSTRUCTIONS

Note

The flight limitations and restrictions on this airplane are subject to change and the latest service instructions and technical orders must be consulted.

1. BEFORE ENTERING THE PILOT'S COMPARTMENT.

a. OUTSIDE THE AIRPLANE.—Check to see that all engine covers, enclosure covers, etc., are removed and properly stowed.

If airplane is on land, check to see wheel chocks are in place. Check to see that nose wheel is in a straight line with the keel. If airplane is moved during preparation for flight, repeat this check.

Check tires and shock struts for proper inflation. Main wheel tires should be inflated to 55 pounds; nose wheel tire to 43 pounds. Strut extension should be 2¾ inches for loadings up to 34,000 pounds.

See that all ice and snow is removed from wing and tail surfaces.

See that pitot head covers are removed. If pitot heads are iced over, turn on pitot heaters.

Entrance to the airplane on either land or water is gained through the waist gun blisters, which may be secured with padlocks. A step aft of each blister is held flush with the hull by a spring. For use, the step may be pulled out and latched in the extended position by turning counterclockwise a quarter turn. A rear entrance ladder, which is hung over the side at the blister, is stowed inside, and may be used after initial entrance is gained.

b. INSIDE THE AIRPLANE.—If the airplane is entered at night, the waist gun compartment light switch, on the forward bulkhead to the left of the door, should be tried. Light will go on if batteries have been left connected to a power bus and the line switch for the aft compartment lights is on the same bus. Otherwise, no lights or electrical equipment will operate until someone goes forward to the radio operator-navigator's compartment to set up the main bus circuits on the power distribution panel. Turn all line switches for all equipment to proper bus.

Soon after coming aboard, the auxiliary power unit should be started. This will insure ample power supply for lights, radio, cooking, etc. When auxiliary power unit is started, be sure to open compartment ventilators overhead, and see that they are left open until time for take-off.

If the airplane has been out of service for several hours, search hull interior for signs of leaks. Any accumulated bilgewater should be bailed out by use of the bilge pump and hose. (See Section I, Part 9).

Check gross weight and c.g. location for take-off and for anticipated loading for landing. Stow loose gear and station crew as necessary for proper balance. Loading data are furnished in the Handbook of Weight and Balance Data, AN 01-1B-40, and supplemented by a Load Adjuster.

Check to see that nothing interferes with movement of controls. Secure all loose gear.

OVERLOAD CAUTION

(1) Do not exceed maximum allowable load.

(2) Do not move CG so far as to endanger control or stability.

(3) Stow load so as to prevent shifting, or interference with controls.

(4) Avoid concentrated loads on portions of structure not designed to bear them (i. e. flooring, midpoints of truss members, etc.)

(5) Avoid overloading plane or landing gear unless operating from smooth runway.

(6) Following rough water operations, particularly at gross weights in excess of 29,000 pounds, careful inspections should be made for any material damage.

Check fuel and oil quantity. Three switches must be operated to read oil tank liquidometer. The line switch on the power distribution panel marked "OIL GAGE" must be on the proper bus. The energizing switch next to the selector switch on the engineer's instrument panel must be "ON." The selector switch must be set for right or left tank readings, as desired.

Section II
Paragraph 1-2

AN 01-5MA-1

Turn on oxygen cylinder valves and read pressure gages. Recharge or replace any cylinder in which the pressure is less than 1800 ± 50 pounds. Check condition of oxygen face masks and tubes for leaks or obstructions. (See Section V, Paragraph 2.)

Check supply of fluid in hydraulic system reservoir (Specification AN-VV-O-366) and in propeller anti-icer fluid reservoir. Check supply of fluid in windshield spray reservoir.

Check supply of oil in auxiliary power unit oil tank.

Check batteries with hydrometer and voltmeter. Hydrometer reading should be 1250 or more. Voltage should be 24 volts or more.

Check condition of all fire extinguishers in the airplane. Check fuel tank vapor dilution system to see if CO_2 cylinders are fully charged and red blow-out disks are intact.

Check supply of spare lamps and fuses.

Check food and water stowage, first aid kits, life jackets, life raft, parachutes, smoke grenades and float lights.

Check supply of chemical toilet bags and toilet paper.

Make ground checks of radar, radio, and interphone equipment.

Be sure power switch for remote compass indicators is on, and that both dials are giving same reading.

Check ammunition supply and flares. Be sure that flare tube doors operate properly.

Check condition of water seals on gun blisters.

Check all transparent windows and enclosures for good visibility.

See that tail anti-icer air scoop is closed. (Push handle on bulkhead 7 all the way in).

Examine all log books to see if entries are up to date.

See that all cowling is properly fastened and that all inspection doors and covers are secured.

Check for presence of engine handcrank.

2. ON ENTERING THE PILOT'S COMPARTMENT.

Unlock surface controls and stow control yoke locking bar. Check controls for freedom of action.

Switch on all the pilot-engineer signal lights, first from the pilot's control yoke, then from the engineer's instrument panel, and check for burned-out lamps. Set interphone control switch in position No. 4.

Switch landing gear indicator light to "INDICATE" momentarily, for check.

Make the following special checks if night flying is contemplated:

Test every light on the airplane by switching on momentarily. Check to see that all line switches or circuit breakers for lights are on.

Check for burned out fuses and bulbs.

Check flares in racks.

Check signal pistol stowage and ammunition.

Check to see that blackout curtains are available for all windows.

Check for spare fluorescent light tubes.

Check instrument dials for condition of luminous markings.

Make sure there is at least one flashlight aboard.

Make check of all radio and interphone controls in pilot's compartment.

Be sure gyropilot is turned off.

Adjust tab settings according to loading.

Work engine controls to check for freedom of action, and leave set in proper positions for starting engines, as follows:

Propellers—Maximum rpm position.

Cowl Flaps—Open.

Mixture Control—"IDLE CUT-OFF."

Throttles—Approximately 1/5 open.

Order airplane headed into the wind. If airplane is on land, set parking brake before starting engines. Check hydraulic system pressure gage to be sure there is at least 800 pounds pressure for brakes.

CAUTION

If airplane is on land, do not allow nose wheel to be turned more than 30° left or right. When airplane is in take-off position, nose wheel should be directly in line with keel, so that airplane will roll straight ahead when power is applied, and maneuvering with brakes and engines to straighten out nose wheel will not be necessary. See that wheel chocks are in proper position.

Check all instruments for proper pointer position, loose, broken or dirty cover glasses. Clean with soft cloth.

Set altimeter to station altitude.

Set rate of climb indicator to zero.

Wind and set all clocks and navigation watches.

Check air speed indicator to see that pointer indicates zero, or value of wind velocity component in direction of aircraft heading.

Before engines are started, check for air in gyropilot hydraulic system. Engage gyropilot and attempt

AN 01-5MA-1

Section II
Paragraph 2-3

to move manual controls. Controls should NOT be resilient (springy), when a moderate pressure is applied.

Note

Do not mistake stretching of cables for air in the hydraulic system. If in doubt, note whether there is any movement of the follow-up indices of the control units when pressure is applied.

Operate windshield wiper to be sure that it works.
Check stowage of emergency landing gear "DOWN. LATCH" lever.

3. FUEL SYSTEM MANAGEMENT.
(See figure 30.)

a. DESCRIPTION.—The wing center section contains two integrally built sealed chambers with a total usable fuel capacity of 1750 U. S. gallons. (1457 Imperial gallons.)

(1) SELF-SEALING CELLS.—Provision is made for installation of self-sealing cells in either or both of the two chambers. A tank dumping and vapor dilution system is installed in the integral tanks.

The fuel tank plan provides for installation of five self-sealing cells in the starboard tank of all odd numbered airplanes, and in the port tank of all even numbered airplanes as they leave the factory. Cells can be installed, however, in both tanks, or may be completely removed, as required. The cells fit into the tank (left or right) for which they are designed, and are not interchangeable.

When cells are installed on one side, the maximum capacity of the cells plus the remaining integral tank is 1497 U. S. gallons. (1242.5 Imperial gallons). When cells are installed in both tanks, the maximum capacity (water-borne) is 1244 U. S. gallons. (1032.5 Imperial gallons).

(2) SELECTOR VALVES.—The fuel flow from the tanks to the engines is controlled by the selector valves on the engineer's panel. The valves are controlled by pointer handles, which indicate their setting on dials. The port valve can be set to feed fuel from either or both tanks to the port engine. The starboard valve can be set to feed fuel from either or both tanks to the starboard engine.

(3) HAND WOBBLE PUMPS.—Connected to the selector valves, and also mounted on the engineer's panel are the A.E.L. units, incorporating strainers and the two hand wobble pumps. The wobble pump handles are so designed that both pumps can be operated simultaneously with one hand, or separately, as desired.

(4) STRAINERS AND DRAINS.—The strainers are provided with drain cocks, with controls on the engineer's panel, so that they may be drained during flight.

(5) AUXILIARY POWER UNIT CENTRAL HEATER AND TAIL ANTI-ICER FUEL SUPPLY. —A separate selector valve for the auxiliary power unit fuel supply and the tail anti-icer fuel supply is located at the lower right-hand corner of the engineer's panel. The fuel line to the central heater system is also served by the same selector valve.

(6) FLOWMETERS.—Two direct-indicating type flowmeters, with by-pass controls are mounted at the top of the engineer's control panel.

Fuel flow rate through the meters is indicated by the calibrated scales on each side of the transparent tubes. The calibrations on the left-hand scale of each flowmeter indicate gallons per hour based on the use of aviation grade gasoline, specific gravity 0.71 at a temperature of 39°C (102°F). The right-hand scale is calibrated to read pounds per hour. The gallons per hour scale is accurate only at the temperature and specific gravity given above.

The float, or flow indicator within the tube, rises as the rate of flow increases, or drops as the rate of flow decreases, to give the rate readings.

The by-pass valve and handle on each flowmeter permits complete isolation of the meter from the fuel system. When the by-pass valve handle is pulled out, fuel passes directly from the inlet port to the outlet port. When the handle is pushed in, the flow is directed through the flowmeter and flow rate is indicated by the float.

(7) PRIMER.—Engine priming is accomplished by means of a hand priming pump on the port side of the engineer's compartment.

(8) ENGINE-DRIVEN PUMPS.—When the engines are running, fuel pressure is supplied by the two engine-driven pumps. Each pump has a relief valve set to short-circuit fuel flow from the discharge port directly back to the intake port, when the fuel pressure rises higher than approximately 18 pounds per square inch.

(9) CROSS-FEED.—A cross-feed system is provided for use in case of failure of either of the engine-driven pumps. The cross-feed valve makes it possible to direct fuel from the one functioning pump to the carburetors on both engines. If one engine fails, fuel can be directed from either one or both tanks to the live engine by use of the cross-feed system.

(10) DRAIN AND REFUEL PROVISIONS.— Tank drain and refuel lines are installed in both integral tanks. They can be used only when fuel cells are not installed in the tanks. By attaching a one-inch pipe

Section II

AN 01-5MA-1

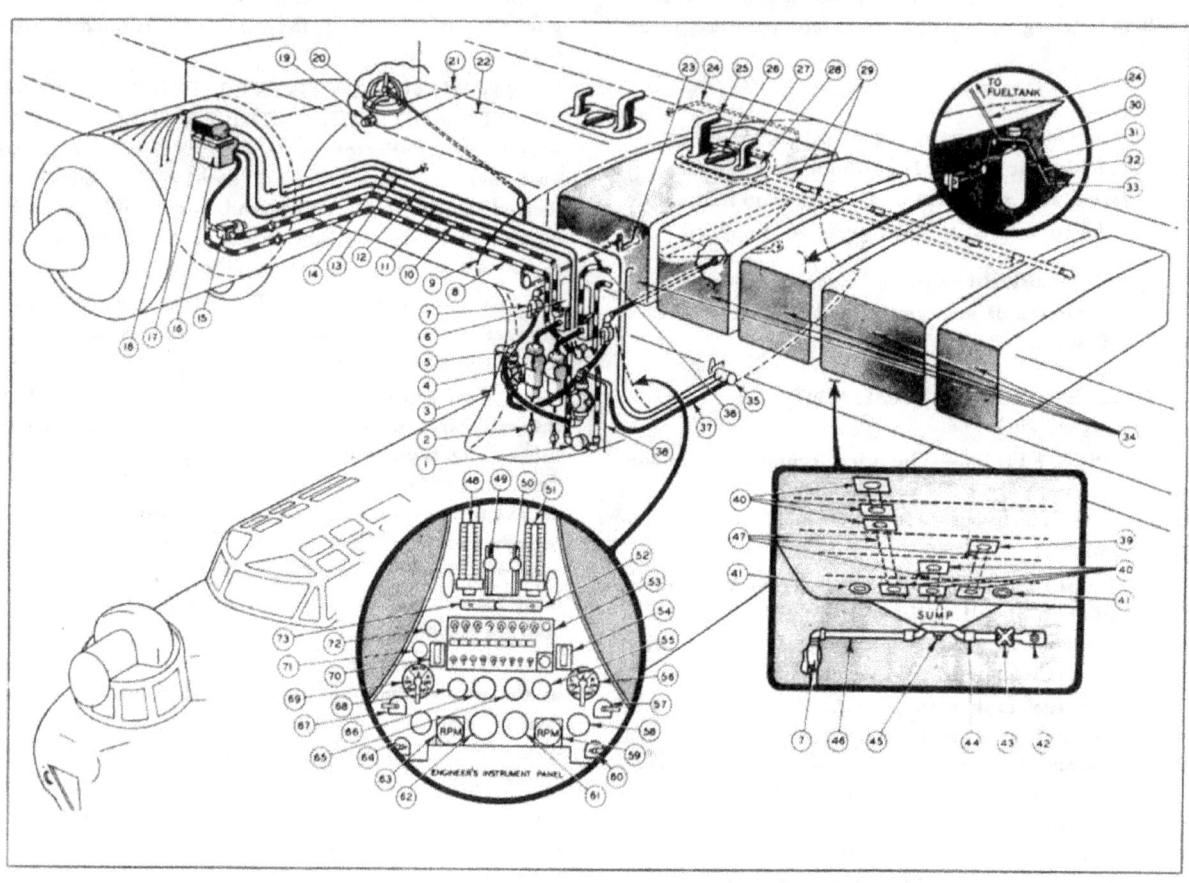

1. Cross-feed Selector Valve
2. Strainer Drain Valve
3. Aux Power Unit Fuel Line
4. A.E.L. Unit
5. Fuel Selector Cock
6. Flowmeter
7. Main Fuel Shut-off Valve
8. Cross-feed Fuel Line
9. Center Line of Wing
10. Main Fuel Line to Engine
11. Fuel Pressure Line
12. Vent Line to Pressure Gage
13. Engine Primer Line
14. Vent Line—Tank to Carburetor
15. Engine-Driven Fuel Pump
16. Carburetor
17. Carburetor Elbow Scoop
18. Primer Line Spider
19. Check Valve—Dump Duct
20. Dump Valve
21. Dump Duct
22. Integral Fuel Tank
23. Dump Valve Control Lever

24. Vapor Dilution Line
25. Vent Stand Pipe—S.S. Cells
26. Filler Neck Cover
27. Vent Stand Pipe—Tank
28. Fuel Tank Manhole Cover
29. S.S. Cells Vent Tubes
30. Purging Cylinder Pull Handle
31. Purging Cylinder
32. Pressure-Relief Line
33. Pressure Relief Disk
34. Self-Sealing Fuel Cells
35. Primer Pump
36. Dump Valve Control Cable
37. Fuel Line to Primer Pump
38. Fuel Line to Central Heater
39. Fuel Cell Manifold Inspection Window
40. Fuel Cell Manifold Access Doors
41. Sight Gage Inspection Window
42. Main Tank Drain Outlet
43. Shut-off Valve—Tank Drain
44. Main Tank Drain & Refueling
45. Sump Drain Plug
46. Main Fuel Line From Sump
47. S.S. Cell Manifold Lines
48. Port Flowmeter

49. Port Fuel Mixture Control
50. Starboard Fuel Mixture Control
51. Starboard Flowmeter
52. Starboard Wobble Pump Handle
53. Engineer-Pilot Visual Signal Panel
54. Starboard Carbtr Air Control
55. Starboard Eng Cyl Temp Gage
56. Starboard Fuel Selector
57. Aux Power Unit Selector
58. Starboard Eng Manifold Pressure Gage
59. Starboard Tachometer
60. Starboard Strainer Drain Selector
61. Starboard Fuel & Oil Pressure Gage
62. Port Fuel & Oil Pressure Gage
63. Port Tachometer
64. Cross-feed Selector
65. Oil Quantity Gage
66. Altimeter
67. Port Strainer Drain Selector
68. Port Eng Cyl Temp Gage
69. Port Fuel Selector
70. Port Carburetor Air Control
71. Outside Air Temp Gage
72. Clock
73. Port Wobble Pump Handle

Figure 30—Fuel System Diagram

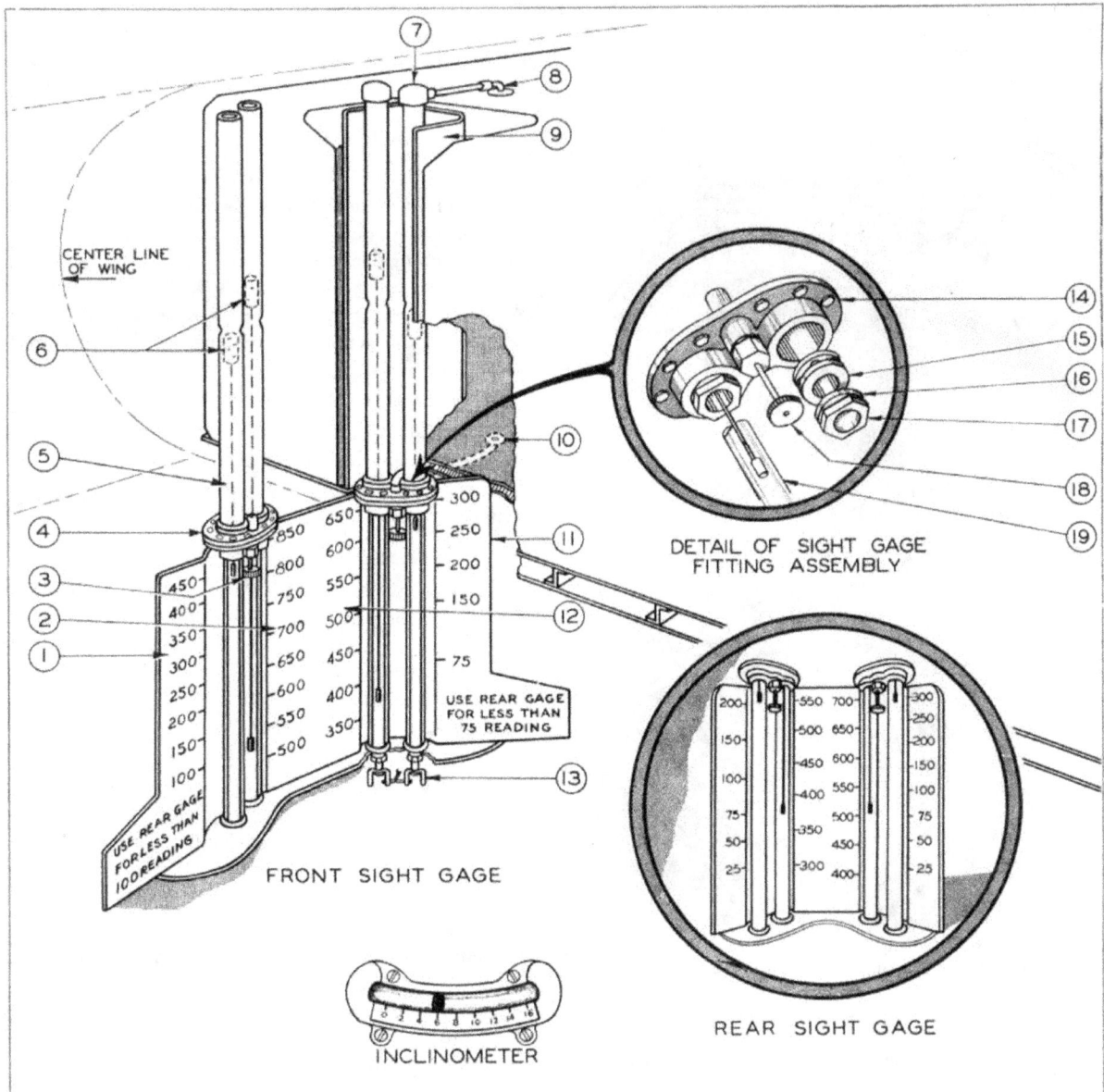

Figure 31—Fuel Sight Gage

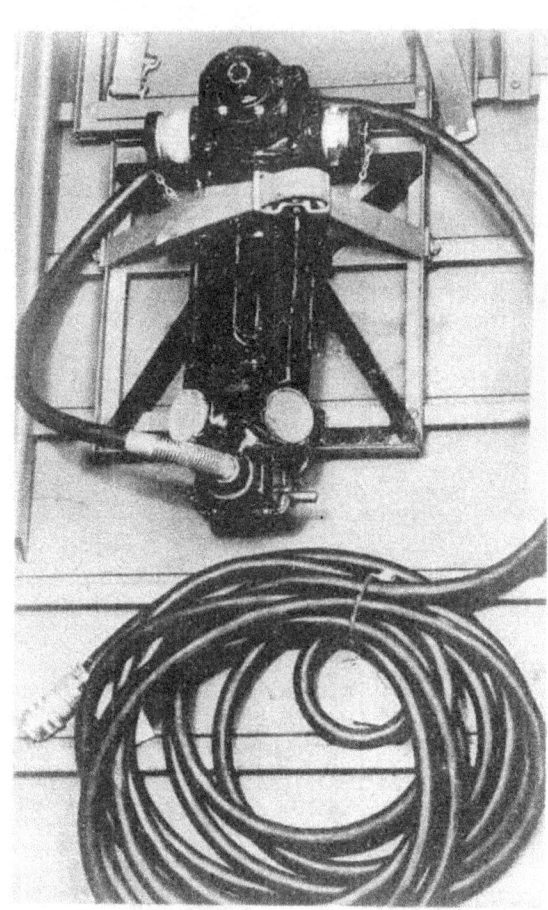

Figure 32—Portable Refueling Pump

fitting to the outer terminal of either drain line, the line can be used for pressure refueling. The drain shut-off valves are incorporated in the A.E.L. units mentioned previously, and the valve control handles are near the bottom of the engineer's instrument panel, on both sides.

(11) FUEL DUMPING PROVISIONS.—Each airplane is equipped with a dump valve and duct by means of which fuel in the integral tank may be dumped quickly. The valve is operated by a lever and cable. The lever is located directly over the engineer's head. Fuel can be dumped only from integral tanks. Dump valves and ducts are installed on the starboard sides of all even numbered airplanes, and on the port sides of all odd numbered airplanes.

Each dump valve and duct system is equipped with vapor dilution provisions, consisting of a carbon dioxide cylinder, a pull handle, and the necessary tubing to carry the carbon dioxide gas into the tank. The pull handle is mounted immediately aft and to the right of the engineer's seat.

(12) FUEL SIGHT GAGES. *(See figure 31.)*—Fuel quantity is indicated by the two sets of sight gages. One pair is under the wing front spar, immediately aft of the engineer's instrument panel. The other pair is under the wing rear spar, aft of the engineer's seat. An inclinometer to guide the engineer in making corrections to the sight gage readings at different longitudinal attitudes of the airplane is located on the starboard side of the engineer's compartment.

(13) FUEL PRESSURE GAGES.—Fuel pressure is indicated by the fuel pressure gages which form parts of the two engine gage units on the engineer's instrument panel.

b. OPERATION.

(1) READING THE FUEL SIGHT GAGES.—The fuel sight gages are calibrated to show the quantity of fuel in U. S. gallons. When self-sealing cells are installed, the calibration for the gages attached to the cell side of the wing will differ from the calibrations on the gages for the opposite tank.

The two inside gage tubes show fuel quantities in the tanks from full to half full. Readings are calibrated at the center of the gage plate for the inside tubes. The two outside tubes indicate fuel quantities from the half full to empty ranges. Readings are taken from the outside calibrations on the plate.

Gage scales are calibrated to read correctly the contents of tanks or cells when the airplane is at an angle of 3½ degrees to the chord line. The rear gage only is to be used after fuel has dropped to 100 gallons in the integral tank, or 75 gallons in the cells.

Use of the inclinometer, mounted on the starboard side of the engineer's compartment, and use of the tilt charts above the inclinometer, are required to make accurate readings of the sight gages.

EXAMPLE

Forward gage reads 500 gallons. Rear gage reads 600 gallons. Inclinometer shows airplane tilted at 7°. Tilt chart for front gage shows correction (for 500 gallons reading at 7° tilt) is 545 gallons. Tilt chart for rear gage shows correction for 600 gallons (reading at 7° tilt) is 545 gallons also. Actual quantity of fuel is, therefore, 545 gallons.

AN 01-5MA-1

Section II
Paragraph 3

(2) FLOWMETER OPERATION.—For normal operation the flowmeters are always by-passed. (By-pass valve handles pulled out.) The by-pass valve handles are pushed on only long enough to take a reading. For normal consumption rate of fuel under various flight conditions, see Cruising Control Chart, Figure 64.

(3) OPERATION OF FUEL SELECTOR VALVES.—The various combinations of tank-to-engine fuel flow are shown on the Fuel Selector Valve Position Chart. *(See figure 33.)*

(4) OPERATION OF CROSS-FEED SYSTEM.—The various combinations of fuel selector valve setting with only one fuel pump operating and the cross-feed valve "ON" are shown on the Fuel Selector Valve Position Chart. *(See figure 33.)* The cross-feed valve should always be "OFF" except in case of engine or fuel pump failure.

(5) OPERATION OF HAND WOBBLE PUMPS.—The hand wobble pumps are used to furnish fuel pressure to start the engines, and to furnish emergency pressure in case one of the engine-driven fuel pumps is disabled.

(6) OPERATION OF PRIMING PUMP.—The hand priming pump is on the port side of the engineer's compartment. The pump handle can be turned to select the engine to be primed. To unlock the plunger, push the handle all the way down; turn to right or left "ON," as desired. Plunger may then be pulled back for the stroke.

Before priming an engine, bring the fuel pressure up to 15 pounds per square inch with the hand wobble pump. Number of priming strokes required for starting will vary from no prime with a hot engine to six or eight, or more, strokes with very cold engines. Excessive priming will load the cylinders with raw gasoline, making it difficult to start the engine. Underpriming is usually indicated by backfiring of the engine through the intake system, with attendant hazards.

Always make certain that the primer pump is locked in "OFF" position before engine is started. A vacuum check prevents suction of fuel into the engine if the primer is accidentally left in the "ON" position, but the engineer should check to see that the plunger is locked "OFF" as a safety precaution. To shut off, push the handle all the way in and turn to "OFF."

(7) MIXTURE CONTROL.—The engines are equipped with Bendix-Stromberg carburetors of the PD-12H4 series, having automatic mixture control which may be set for "FULL RICH," "AUTOMATIC RICH," "AUTOMATIC LEAN" or "IDLE CUT-OFF."

The usual operating position is "AUTO RICH." In this position the mixture control automatically maintains desired fuel/air ratios at all engine speeds and loads, independent of changes in altitude, temperature, propeller pitch, supercharger speed or throttle position.

The "AUTOMATIC LEAN" position provides a leaner mixture for cruising economy. This setting may be too lean for good acceleration. Therefore, when maneuvers are necessary, or when changing engine power, use "AUTOMATIC RICH."

Intermediate positions on the mixture control quadrant may also be used. Between positions there is a fairly uniform transition in effect upon the mixture being delivered to the carburetor. Between "FULL RICH" and "AUTOMATIC RICH" the transition varies in its rate and amount depending upon the density of the air entering the carburetor as affected by temperature and altitude. "AUTOMATIC LEAN" is 5% to 10% leaner than "AUTOMATIC RICH," depending upon the particular carburetor setting. Between "AUTOMATIC LEAN" and "IDLE CUT-OFF" further reduction in mixture strength is attainable by manual control. Extreme caution must be exercised when setting mixture control beyond "AUTOMATIC LEAN," with due regard to engine operating conditions and fuel characteristics.

Before cruising in "AUTOMATIC LEAN" the engines should be cooled down to 232°C (450°F). Refer to the Specific Engine Flight Chart, Figure 38, for recommended manifold pressures and rpm settings to be used for cruising in "AUTOMATIC LEAN."

CAUTION

Fuel will flow through the carburetor when the mixture control is in any position except "IDLE CUT-OFF" whenever the fuel pressure is greater than five pounds per square inch, whether the engine is running or stopped. The mixture control should, therefore, be left in "IDLE CUT-OFF" position whenever engines are stopped.

(8) FUEL SPECIFICATION.—The engine calibrations and flight operating data in this handbook are based on fuel of Specification AN-F-28 (Grade 100/130). The self sealing cells and hoses installed are resistant to aromatic fuel compounds.

(9) FUEL DUMPING PROCEDURE.—The vapor dilution pull handle must be pulled immediately after fuel dumping is completed. It is important that there be no delay, as the fire hazard of the fuel vapor is great. Once the dilution handle is pulled, the CO_2 cylinder will be completely discharged, and must be replaced or recharged before another dumping operation can be performed.

WARNING

Do not smoke while fuel is being dumped. Close all hull vents and blisters. Shut down all electrical equipment, radio, APU, float motors, etc.

Section II

AN 01-5MA-1

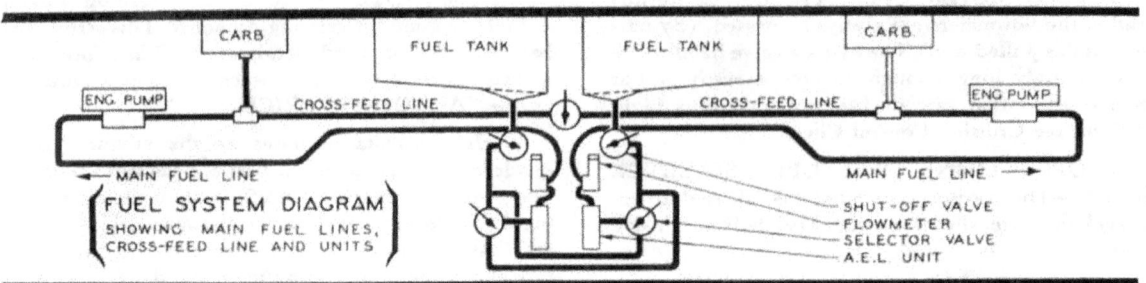

FUEL CONTROL POSITIONS WITH CROSS-FEED VALVE "OFF"

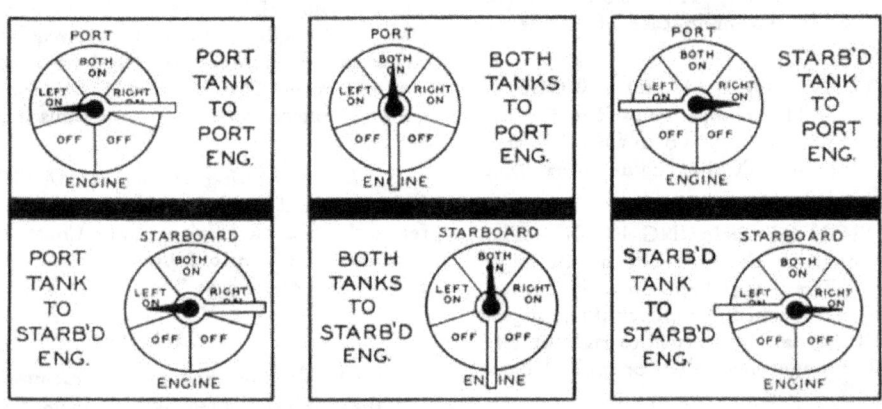

FUEL CONTROL POSITIONS WITH CROSS-FEED VALVE "ON"
(NOTE: CROSS-FEED VALVE TO BE "ON" ONLY IF PUMP FAILS.)

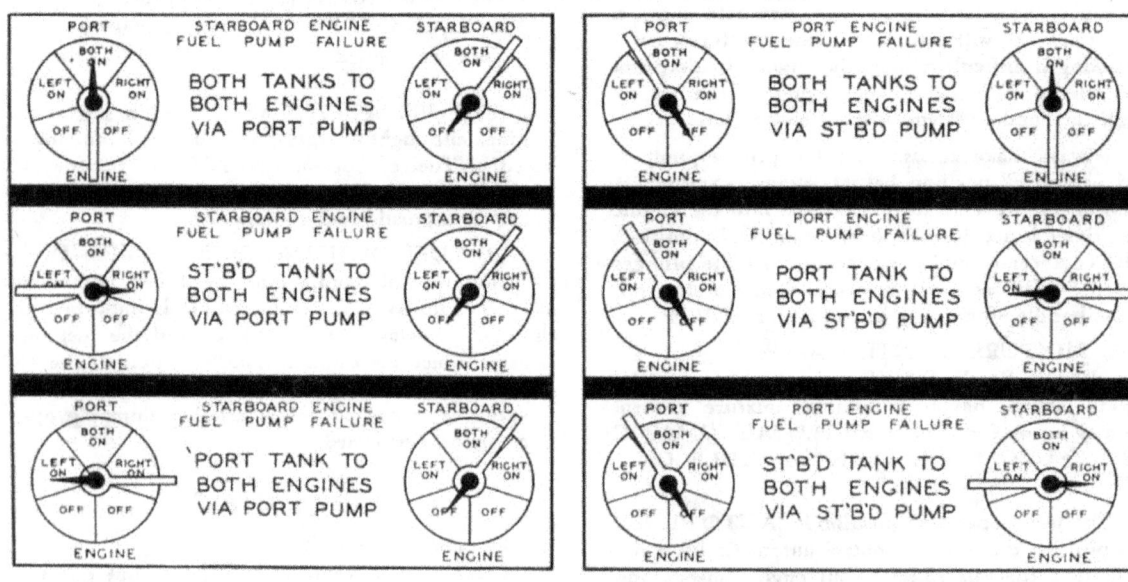

Figure 33—Fuel Selector Valve Position Chart

44

4. STARTING ENGINES.

CAUTION

Auxiliary power unit should be running and unit generator and battery line switches should be on the same bus when engines are started. Main generator and battery switches should be off.

PILOT

a. Request radioman to start auxiliary power unit and to check main distribution panel for proper setting of main bus switches, proper voltmeter and ammeter readings for auxiliary power unit, etc.

c. Set vacuum selector valve so starboard engine runs gyro instruments, and gyropilot vacuum line is on port engine.

d. Propellers—Highest rpm position.

e. Throttle—One fifth open.

j. Ignition Switches—Both "ON."

q. Throttle—If engine is flooded, open throttle wide at request from engineer.

CAUTION

Be prepared to retard throttle quickly in case engine fires. If engineer opens mixture control and resumes pumping with wobble pump, engine might run away if throttles are open.

FLIGHT ENGINEER

b. Set fuel valves for "LEFT ON" and "RIGHT ON."

f. Start starboard engine first because hydraulic system pump is on this engine. Turn engine over several revolutions by hand to clear bottom cylinders. (It is advisable to remove the lower spark plugs if there is reason to believe the bottom cylinders are loaded).

g. Carburetor Air—"DIRECT."

h. Mixture Control—"IDLE CUT-OFF."

i. Cowl Flaps—"OPEN."

k. Priming.—With the hand wobble pump, bring fuel pressure up to 15 pounds per square inch. Prime engine with primer pump. Six to eight strokes of the primer pump may be necessary if engine is cold.

l. Starter—Maintain fuel pressure at eight to ten pounds with wobble pump and turn right engine starter switch to "START." Hold switch in this position until inertia drive comes up to speed, (approximately ten seconds) then move switch to "MESH."

m. Mixture Control—"IDLE CUT-OFF" while starter is turning engine over. "AUTO RICH" as soon as engine fires.

n. Fuel Pressure—Maintain eight to ten pounds pressure with hand wobble pump.

o. Failure to Start—If engine does not start almost immediately, (three seconds) leave mixture control in "IDLE CUT-OFF." Repeat use of hand primer and wobble pump.

p. Flooded Engine—Flooding is generally indicated by a discharge of fuel from the engine blower case drain, or by presence of raw gasoline in the exhaust. To clear engine, discontinue use of wobble pump, request pilot to open throttle wide, and turn engine over several revolutions by moving starter switch to "MESH" intermittently.

Section II
Paragraph 4-5

AN 01-5MA-1

PILOT

s. Throttle—As soon as engine starts, adjust throttle to as low a speed as possible for the first 30 seconds after starting. Stand by for engineer's report on oil pressure.

v. Throttle—After the first half minute, adjust the throttle to about 1000 rpm.

5. ENGINE WARM-UP AND ACCESSORY CHECK.
a. Propeller—Leave in highest rpm position.

c. Throttle—Set for about 1000 rpm.

g. Throttle—Set for approximately 30 in. Hg when oil temperature has reached 40°C (104°F).

i. Ignition Switches—Check rpm drop when switching from "BOTH" to "R" or "L" magneto. Normal drop is 50 to 75 rpm and should not exceed 100 rpm. After checking one magneto, switch to "BOTH" for a few seconds before checking the other magneto. Make magneto check in as short a time as practicable, so that detonation does not cause damage to engine. Check center (emergency) switch momentarily off.

j. Set throttle for 600 rpm and propeller in high rpm position.

l. Throttle—Set for 2000 rpm and request engineer to check engine instruments. Because engine cooling on the ground is usually insufficient at this speed, instrument check should be made in as short a time as possible.

FLIGHT ENGINEER

r. Fuel Pressure—As soon as engine starts, move mixture control to "AUTO RICH." Continue to operate wobble pump vigorously until the engine runs smoothly, and automatically builds up fuel pressure to 14 to 16 pounds per square inch.

t. Oil Pressure—If oil pressure does not register on the gage almost immediately, STOP ENGINES and investigate.

u. Primer—Be sure primer pump handle is locked after engine has started.

b. Cowl Flaps—Leave open under all conditions. Do not attempt to accelerate warm-up by closing cowl flaps. This will cause uneven expansion of cylinders and possible burning of spark plug elbows.

d. Carburetor Air—"DIRECT," unless there is danger of icing, or unless sand or dust is blowing.

e. Oil Pressure—When starts are made with cold oil, oil pressure may go as high as 300 pounds for a minute or more while the delayed action of the compensating relief valve is controlled by the temperature of the incoming oil. The high pressure is reduced when the oil inlet temperature reaches 40°C (104°F). Desired oil pressure, 65 to 105 pounds per square inch at 1500 rpm.

f. If on land, check to be sure floats are up and locked. If on water, check to see that landing gear is up and locked and that nose wheel door is locked.

h. Oil Temperature—Report to pilot when oil temperature reaches 40°C (104°F).

k. Make idle mixture check with throttle set for 600 rpm. Move the mixture control lever smoothly and steadily into the "IDLE CUT-OFF" position and observe the tachometer for any change in rpm. Return the mixture control lever to the "AUTO RICH" position before the engine cuts out. A rise of more than 10 rpm indicates too rich an idle mixture, and no change or a drop in rpm indicates that the mixture is too lean. A rise of 5 to 10 rpm is recommended in order to permit idling at low speeds without danger of fouling plugs and at the same time to afford good acceleration characteristics.

PILOT

p. Hydraulic Pressure Gage—Should read 800 to 1000 pounds pressure.

q. Propellers—After 2000 rpm check, pull throttles back to approximately 1000 rpm and pull propeller governor control back to extreme high pitch. (Low rpm.) Move slowly forward again to extreme low pitch. (High rpm.) Check operation of feathering mechanism by feathering and unfeathering once.

s. Automatic Pilot—If only one engine is running, check vacuum selector valve to be sure that gyropilot is on the vacuum pump that is running, then check gyropilot as follows:

(1) Check vacuum gage. Should read 3.75 to 5 inches Hg.

(2) See that four-way oil valve, to pilot's left, is "ON," and oil pressure gage shows pressure. (150 pounds at 1000 rpm engine speed.)

(3) Uncage bank and climb gyro. (Turn caging knob clockwise as far as it will go.)

(4) Set and uncage directional gyro control. (Push caging knob in and turn to set lower card to desired heading, then pull knob out.)

(5) Turn rudder knob on directional gyro control to align upper card with lower card.

(6) Turn aileron knob until follow-up index on top of bank and climb gyro dial matches zero point on banking scale.

Note

If airplane is on the water, one float or the other will be down and the airplane will be tilted laterally the number of degrees indicated by the inclinometer under the directional gyro. Aileron index should be set for same number of degrees deflection.

(7) Turn elevator knob until the follow-up index matches the elevator alignment index at the side of the bank and climb gyro dial.

CAUTION

Do not align follow-up index with the horizon bar.

FLIGHT ENGINEER

m. Oil Pressure—Should be 85 pounds + 15 — 5 pounds at 2000 rpm.

n. Fuel Pressure—14 to 16 pounds.

o. Cylinder Temperature—Do not exceed 232°C (450°F) during ground check.

r. If there is sufficient time, have canvas scoop rigged to tail anti-icer air scoop, and check operation of tail anti-icer.

t. Warn pilot to discontinue ground check of gyropilot system if engine cylinder temperatures and oil temperatures are rising above safe limits. 260°C (500°F).

PILOT

(8) Make sure that surface controls operate freely and engage gyropilot with "ON-OFF" lever at top of pilot's compartment. Move lever SLOWLY all the way "ON."

(9) Check oil pressure on gage. (Should be 150 pounds ± 10 pounds.)

(10) Check operation of gyropilot by rotating rudder knob each way. The servo speed control valve settings will determine the speed of control.

(11) Check to see if gyropilot can be overpowered manually without excessive force on the controls.

(12) Disengage gyropilot.

(13) Gyro Horizon and Directional Gyro—Check gyro instruments not included in gyropilot control panel. Uncage gyro horizon and check to see that there is no precession, and that instrument's indications will be that of the airplane's position. Set and uncage directional gyro. (See instructions above for directional gyro on gyropilot panel.) Check for instrument drift of not more than 4° in 15 minutes.

(14) Check for air in automatic pilot hydraulic system. Controls should not be resilient (springy) when a moderate pressure is applied to them, but should feel as though locked. If air is present, remove it.

Note

Do not confuse stretching of cable with the presence of air in the hydraulic system. If in doubt, note whether there is any movement of the follow-up indices of the control units. Stretching of the cable will not cause these indices to move.

w. If immediate take-off is contemplated, order all hatches and ventilators secured. If on water, make sure anchor gear is stowed, mooring lines clear, that gun blister water seals are inflated, etc. If on land, see that wheel chocks are removed and that nose wheel is pointed straight ahead. See that entrance ladders are stowed.

x. Determine if continued use of auxiliary power unit will be necessary, and if not, shut off unit.

y. If on land, check to see that floats are up and securely latched. If on water, check to see that floats are securely latched in down position.

z. Check with someone aft to see that tail anti-icer air scoop is closed, and that anti-icer switch is off. See that temporary canvas scoop is removed and stowed.

FLIGHT ENGINEER

u. Request radioman to switch on main engine generators and batteries and to read meters to check for proper power output. (27.5 to 28 volts with no load.)

v. Check operation of galley stove by turning one hot plate on high position and the other on low position and note the difference in heat; then reverse switches and check.

AN 01-5MA-1

Section II
Paragraph 6-7-8

6. EMERGENCY TAKE-OFF.

If oil was diluted when engines were last stopped, take-off may be made as soon as pressure is steady at around 65 to 75 pounds.

If oil was not diluted, the oil dilution valve may be opened intermittently after starting engines, at intervals of a few seconds for a period of about 15 seconds, or until oil pressure is steady.

Be sure propellers are in highest rpm (full low pitch) position.

Leave cowl flaps open. Closing cowl flaps will not assist warm-up, and will damage engine.

Proceed with normal take-off.

7. ENGINE AND ACCESSORIES OPERATION GROUND TEST.

(See No. 5, "ENGINE WARM-UP AND ACCESSORY CHECK").

8. TAXIING INSTRUCTIONS.

a. GENERAL.—Taxiing should not be done at very low or very high rpm. No restriction can be placed on taxiing rpm, but it should be noted that a large part of ignition troubles may be due to overheating the installation by taxiing at high speeds.

Automatic rich mixture is desirable for cool ground operation.

Cowl flaps should be open for all taxiing operations. Ignition troubles at low idling rpm may be due to improper setting of the idle mixture adjustment.

In using engines, a little power applied for longer periods is better than repeated short surges of power, which tend to empty the accelerator pump, if sufficient time is not allowed for the pump to refill.

b. LAND TAXIING.—The landing gear may be used for taxiing from land to water and water to land.

WARNING

Emergency hydraulic pump handle must be in operating position before taxiing.

Taxiing on land should be done without brakes wherever possible, as application of brakes for long periods will cause overheating.

Sudden applications of either brake or power should be avoided, as they tend to jerk the nose wheel around, and may damage the gear.

The nose wheel is free to swivel 30° each way, and the airplane can be turned either way while taxiing at a fast rate, without showing a tendency to ground loop, even in wet weather. However, turns should be anticipated sooner than with conventional gear by speeding the outside motor well before the turn and applying the inside brake easily if necessary.

CAUTION

In making small radius turns, avoid locking inside wheel, with resultant tearing of rubber.

One of the main points to consider in taxiing tricycle installations is to avoid starting movement contrary to the direction in which the nose wheel is turned. Pilots should note the position of the nose wheel before entering the airplane. If it is turned sidewise over 30° or caught in a rut, the wheel should be straightened before attempting to taxi. If turned only a small amount, the pilot should begin his taxiing in the direction the nose wheel points, in order to start it castering. After the nose wheel has begun to caster, the plane may be turned to the desired direction. Pilots should start taxiing with no more than the minimum amount of throttle required to start motion, to avoid applying heavy loads on a canted nose wheel. Particular care must be exercised when operating in muddy ground, soft sand, or deep snow.

The nose wheel is dampened against shimmying, and no shimmy should be tolerated, as it can be cured by proper servicing of the dampers. Before the first land take-off each day, the airplane should be taxied for some distance in a straight line, to be sure the nose wheel has no tendency to shimmy.

The main landing gear is located at approximately 41.6 percent of the mean aerodynamic chord. Center of gravity locations forward of this point obviously will have no tendency to rock the airplane so as to lift the nose wheel off the ground. Brakes should not be used during a take-off run. Course corrections should be made with slight throttle changes.

CAUTION

If the brakes have been used to any great extent prior to taxiing up to the line, it is advisable to allow them to cool before applying the parking brakes.

c. WATER TAXIING.—Water taxiing is possible at higher rpm settings than on land because of the constant drag of the water.

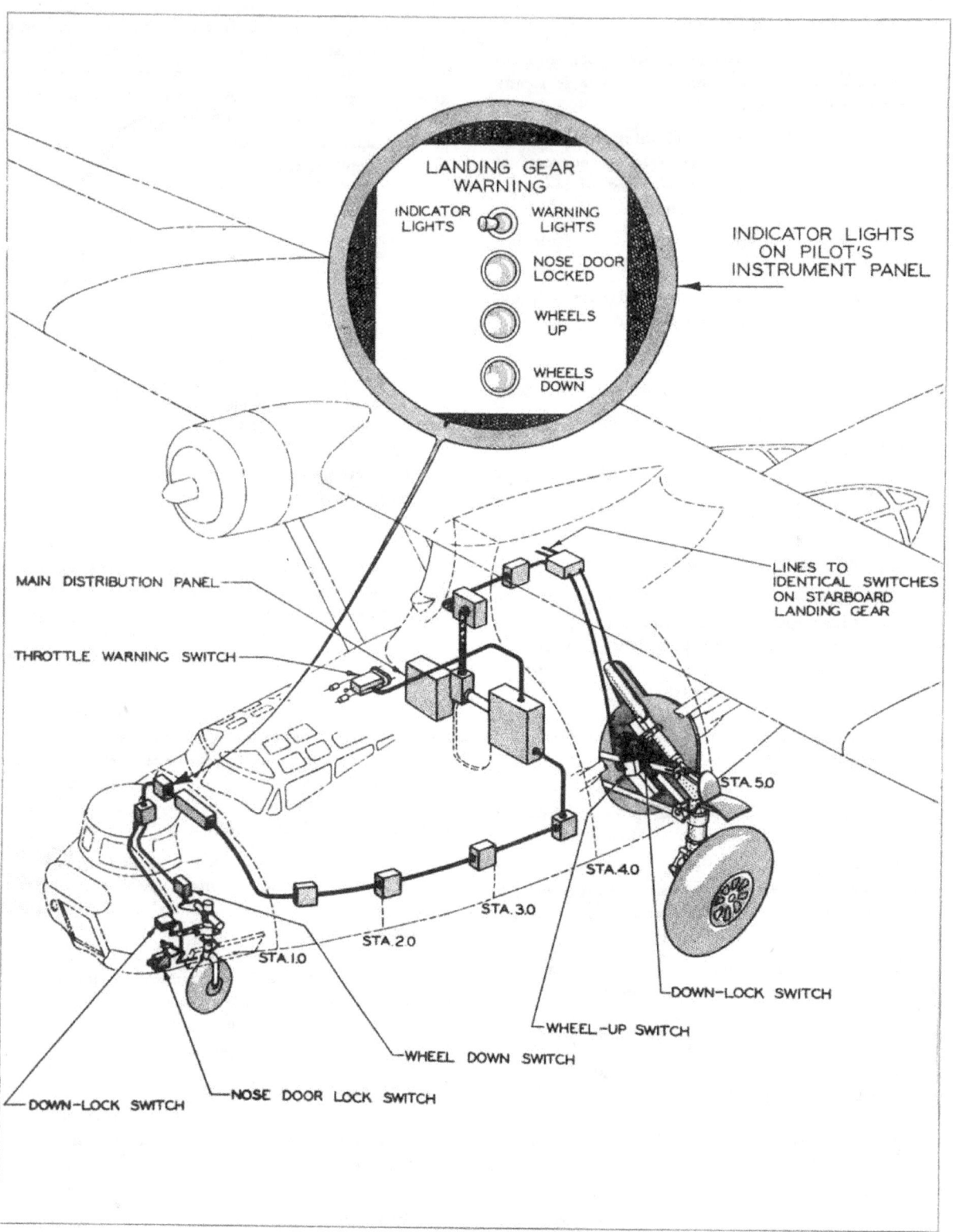

Figure 34—Landing Gear Indicator System

9. TAKE-OFF.

See: Take-Off Check-Off List, Take-Off Climb and Landing Chart and Specific Engine Flight Chart.

a. LAND TAKE-OFF.—Tricycle-geared planes will not take themselves off. When elevator control is gained, the nose wheel should be lifted from the ground, and the run continued on the main wheels until take-off speed is reached.

Best take-off speed is 75 knots.

Maximum recommended gross weight for take-off from average runways is 27,300 pounds; from smooth prepared runways, 34,500 pounds, and from smooth prepared runways with jettisonable load of approximately 2,000 pounds, 36,400 pounds is the maximum recommended gross weight for take-off (LAND TAKE-OFF ONLY). Appropriate reductions of weight must be made for less favorable conditions.

CHECK-OFF LIST—LAND.

PILOT

(1) Check elevator, rudder and aileron tab settings.
(2) Check to make certain rudder control is unlocked and rudder operating freely.
(3) Check automatic pilot "OFF."
(4) Check wing and empennage anti-icers off.

FLIGHT ENGINEER

(5) Check empennage anti-icer ram air duct closed. Check central heater intake air scoop closed.
(6) Check all hatches and openings closed; bomber's window cover down.
(7) Check "FLOATS UP."
(8) Check oil pressure and oil temperature normal.
(9) Mixture Control — Set at "AUTOMATIC RICH."
(10) Carburetor Air Control—Set for "DIRECT" air except when ice or sleet conditions require "ALTERNATE" Setting.
(11) Cowl Flaps—Fully "OPEN" so that cylinder temperature before take-off will not exceed 232°C (450°F).
(12) Report to pilot when ready.

(13) Propellers set for 2700 rpm.
(14) Reduce rpm immediately after take-off to 2550. Maintain 42 in. Hg, or less, manifold pressure.
(15) Raise wheels as soon as possible after take-off.
(16) Check "WHEELS UP" and "WHEEL DOOR LOCKED" by moving indicator light switch to "INDICATE."

(17) COWL FLAPS.—Adjust to maintain cylinder temperature not to exceed 260°C (500°F) for one hour or 232°C (450°F) for continuous cruising; 20°C (68°F) or more below the maximum for each condition is preferred.
(18) If auxiliary power unit is being used, open ventilators in engineer's compartment after take-off is completed.

Section II
Paragraph 9

AN 01-5MA-1

b. WATER TAKE-OFF.

Best take-off speed is between 75 and 80 knots. Maximum recommended gross weight for rough water operation is 27,300 pounds; for smooth water operation, 34,500 pounds is the maximum recommended gross weight for take-off (water take-off only).

CAUTION

Take-off should be accomplished with the minimum spray through props to avoid water entering propeller housing.

CHECK-OFF LIST—WATER.

PILOT

(1) Check elevator, rudder and aileron tab settings.
(2) Check to make certain rudder control is unlocked and rudder operating freely.
(3) Check automatic pilot "OFF."
(4) Check landing gear up and locked by moving indicator light switch to "INDICATE."

(6) Check wing and empennage anti-icers off.

(14) Propellers set 2700 rpm.
(15) Reduce rpm immediately after take-off to 2550. Maintain 42 in. Hg, or less, manifold pressure.

FLIGHT ENGINEER

(5) Check "FLOATS DOWN."

(7) Check empennage anti-icer ram air duct closed.
(8) Check all hatches and openings closed, bomber's window cover down.
(9) Check oil pressure and oil temperature normal. 40°C (104°F) minimum.
(10) Mixture Control—Set at "AUTOMATIC RICH."
(11) Carburetor Air Control—Set for "DIRECT" air except when ice or sleet conditions require "ALTERNATE" setting.
(12) Cowl Flaps—Full "OPEN" so that cylinder temperature before take-off will not exceed 232°C (450°F).
(13) Report to pilot when ready.

(16) COWL FLAPS.—Adjust to maintain cylinder temperature not to exceed 260°C (500°F) for one hour or 232°C (450°F) for continuous cruising; 20°C (68°F) or more below the maximum for each condition is preferred.
(17) If auxiliary power unit is being used, open ventilators in engineer's compartment after take-off is completed.

10. ENGINE FAILURE DURING TAKE-OFF.

In case of engine failure at a low air speed and a low altitude, the pilot must immediately choose between either throttling the remaining engine and landing straight ahead if the ground or water is suitable, or retracting landing gear or floats, carefully building up speed, and continuing in flight until a safe landing can be effected.

If decision is made to land, less damage will probably be done, unless there is a perfect field ahead, if the landing gear is retracted.

If the landing is to be made on good terrain, but in limited space, the airplane should be stalled in, then brought promptly to the three-point attitude and brakes applied. Landings of this type can be made successfully if tires and brakes are in good condition.

If continued flight is undertaken, all maneuvers should be made as gently as possible, to avoid an attitude from which recovery is impossible.

For minimum and best air speed, see Stalling Speed Chart. The pilot must overcome any tendency to pull nose up before sufficient air speed has been obtained.

Where it is necessary to obtain altitude immediately, landing gear or floats should be retracted. However, the hydraulic pump is located on the starboard engine, so failure of that engine will make retraction of the landing gear impossible except by emergency methods requiring approximately five minutes. See "Emergency Operation of Landing Gear." Floats are controlled electrically, so failure of an engine will not affect their operation. Time required to retract floats is 20 seconds.

The airplane must be trimmed (rudder tab first, aileron tab second) for as good a "hands off" condition as possible.

Banks must be made with the dead engine high, and only shallow banks should be attempted.

Feather the useless propeller to reduce the drag. If propeller cannot be feathered, place it in low rpm position to reduce vibration. Sufficient air speed will cause the propeller to windmill and turn the dead engine over fast enough to pump oil for the propeller pitch changing mechanism.

Leave propeller of the useful engine in the high rpm position to give maximum engine power output. Shut off the fuel to the useless engine with the fuel selector valve as soon as practicable. The use of more than rated power at any altitude must be kept to a minimum to avoid overheating and detonation which will result in damage to, if not complete failure of, the remaining engine. The use of rich mixture will help slightly to keep engine cylinder temperatures down.

When landing, rapid settling of the airplane must be anticipated, particularly at the time landing gear or floats are lowered. Before landing is attempted, pilot should gain all the altitude possible, and where practical, simulate landing procedure by lowering wheels or floats and reducing power. Lowering of the wheels by use of the emergency hand pump will require approximately three minutes. See "Emergency Operation of Landing Gear."

11. CLIMB AND HIGH SPEED LEVEL FLIGHT.

For maximum performance (rated power) the propeller should be governed to 2550 rpm, the mixture control set at "AUTOMATIC RICH" and the manifold pressure as given below:

Altitude	Manifold Pressure
Sea Level	42 in. Hg
2500 ft	41 in. Hg
5000 ft	40 in. Hg
7000 ft	39.5 in. Hg
Above 7000 ft	39.5 in. Hg or F. T.

For best rate of climb and indicated air speeds to various altitudes with various gross weights, see Take-Off, Climb and Landing Chart. *(Figure 64.)*

After a long climb, or going to a higher power in cold weather, momentarily reduce the propeller pitch (increase rpm) to permit hot engine oil to clear out the mechanism.

12. GENERAL FLYING CHARACTERISTICS.

The airplane is stable over a wide range of center of gravity locations. However, care should be exercised to operate controls smoothly when flying with the center of gravity near the limits of its range.

At high speeds, the elevators become "heavy," helping to prevent sudden extreme application of the elevator control which might prove damaging to the structure.

Banks up to 60° can be made safely.

It is good practice to slow down to 100 knots in extremely turbulent air.

a. FLIGHT RESTRICTIONS.—Do not exceed an engine speed of 3,060 rpm in a dive 30 seconds maximum duration.

Do not operate automatic pilot when one or more engines are not delivering normal power. It is not necessary to disengage the gyropilot when encountering rough or turbulent air. If necessary, adjust the speed control valves to improve operation. Under extremely turbulent conditions, follow through manually on the controls and assist the gyropilot if necessary.

Do not use the automatic pilot when flying at less than an indicated air speed of 85 knots.

Do not operate the airplane under control of the automatic pilot without at least one rated pilot "on watch."

Restricted speeds and accelerations for gross weights in excess of 26,000 pounds are given in the table below.

Gross Weight (Pounds)	Permissible Acceleration (g's) Positive	Negative	Permissible Speed (Knots-Indicated)
26,000	3.2	1.6	190
28,000	2.9	1.5	175
30,000	2.7	1.4	165
32,000	2.5	1.3	155
34,000	2.3	1.2	145
36,400	2.1	1.1	125

In addition to the above restrictions on acceleration and speed, increasing care in methods of operating at these increased gross weights is considered essential. Such methods often cannot be expressed in figures. For example, turns should be more moderate and all control movements should be smoother.

b. ELEVATOR TRIM.—Five degrees deflection of the elevator trim tab is sufficient to trim the airplane in any power condition, including extended landing gear or floats.

c. CRUISING.—While cruising operations may be conducted at any engine power below normal rated power, in order to obtain low fuel consumption it is recommended that all cruising operations be conducted in a range not to exceed 67 per cent of the normal rated (1050) horsepower. When cruising at above 67 per cent normal rated power, the mixture control should be in the "AUTO RICH" position. When cruising at powers below 67 per cent normal rated power, the mixture control should be in the "AUTO LEAN" position. The cylinder head temperature limit of 232°C (450°F) must not be exceeded during cruising operation.

13. MANEUVERS PROHIBITED.

All maneuvers are prohibited except those prescribed for normal flight.

14. STALLS.

a. STALL CHARACTERISTICS.—With or without power, the airplane settles as it approaches the stall. The stall is very gradual, showing no tendencies to whip.

Indication of approaching stall is a slight tail shake increasing as the stall becomes more evident. Both lateral and directional stability are completely maintained throughout the stall. No shake or loss of control is noticed either in the rudder or aileron. The airplane does not have any severe stalling characteristics. In a normal power-on or power-off stall, the airplane merely mushes down and the recovery is almost instantaneous. However, in more abrupt stalls, a pronounced nose-down fall-off is noticed.

b. STALLING SPEEDS.

(1) CLEAN CONDITION (FLOATS UP—GEAR UP) G. W. 27,000 LBS.

(a) With cowl flaps ¼ open and power off, the indicated stalling speed is approximately 55 knots, with a sinking rate of 300 to 400 ft/min.

(b) With cowl flaps ¼ open and power on, the indicated stalling speed is approximately 53 knots, with a sinking rate of 300 ft/min.

(2) DIRTY CONDITION (FLOATS DOWN—GEAR DOWN).

(a) With cowl flaps ¼ open and power off, the indicated stalling speed is approximately 58 knots with a sinking rate of 400 ft/min.

(b) With cowl flaps ¼ open and power on, the indicated stalling speed is approximately 55 knots, with a sinking rate of 300 ft/min.

In general, the stalling characteristics are very good and require very little effort on the pilot's part during the stall and during recovery. Stalling speeds vary directly with the gross weight of the airplane.

15. SPINS.

This airplane shows no tendency to spin from a slow or steeply banked turn.

When one engine is inoperative, too short a turn toward the dead engine provokes a spin.

If a spin has not progressed too far, recovery may be assisted by increasing power of the engine on the inside of the turn and decreasing power of the engine on the outside of the turn, as well as applying the usual nose-down and opposite aileron and rudder controls. In recovery from a spin, there must be no abrupt movement of the controls.

16. ACROBATICS.

All acrobatics are prohibited in this type of airplane.

17. DIVING.

With a gross weight of 27,000 pounds, airplane must not be pulled out at more than 3 g's.

Maximum engine overspeed is 3060 rpm for 30 seconds.

Place mixture control in "AUTOMATIC RICH" before diving.

Close cowl flaps to prevent too rapid cooling of the engines.

Control trim should be maintained with the idea of keeping tail surface forces to a minimum. Trim the airplane to be slightly nose-heavy in dive, rather than tail-heavy. If airplane were trimmed tail-heavy, there would be an inherent tendency to pull up. This condition might lead to pulling up the elevator too suddenly.

Air loads build up rapidly on a large airplane. For this reason, any abrupt movement of the controls should be avoided.

Note

The limitations and restrictions on this airplane are subject to change and the latest service instructions and applicable technical orders must be consulted.

18. NIGHT FLYING.

Night landings on water should be made with power to avoid a pancake landing in case altitude is misjudged.

Projector lights are provided for night flying, as well as fluorescent and filament lights, and blackout curtains. Projector lights are located in the three forward compartments. Fluorescent lights are located in the bomber's and pilot's compartments. The usual com-

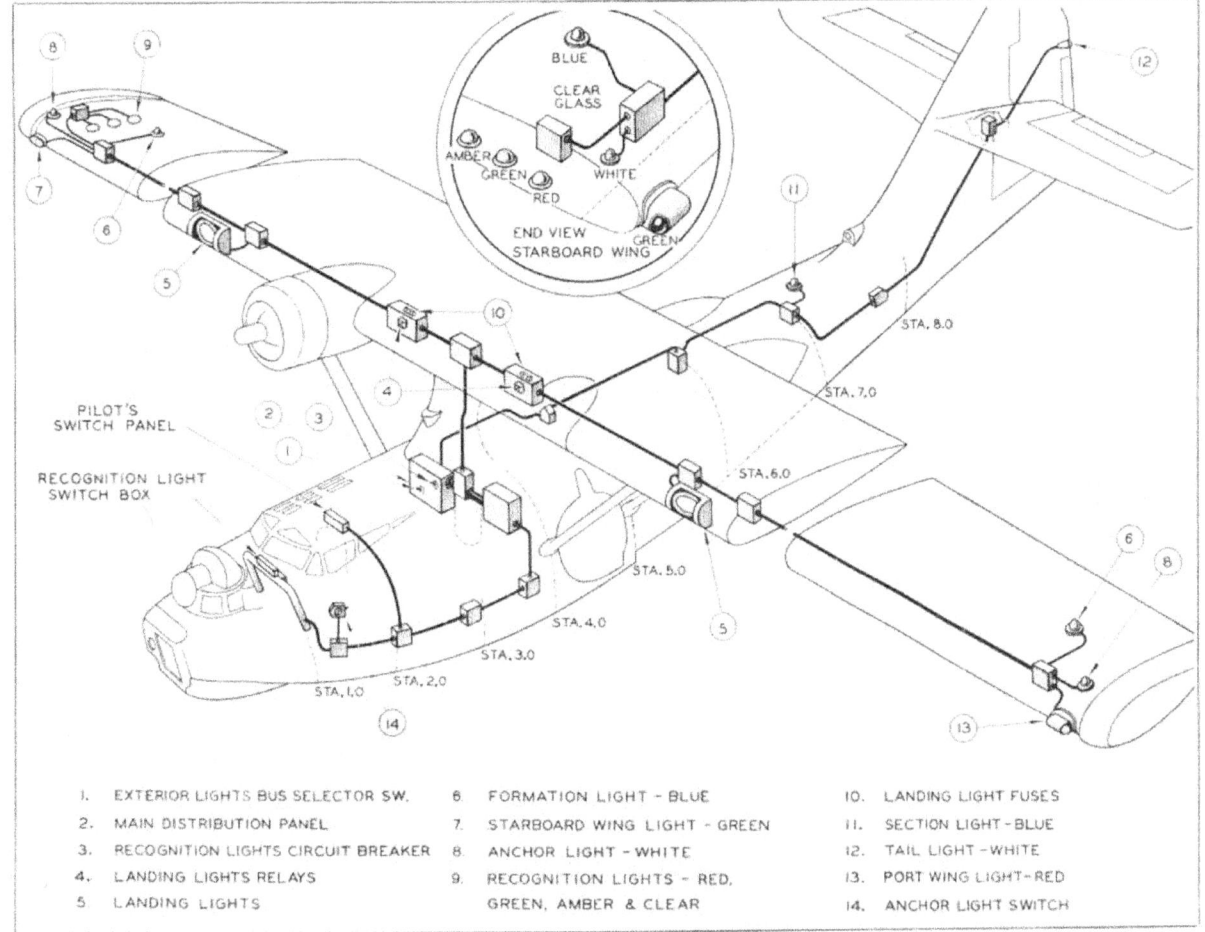

1. EXTERIOR LIGHTS BUS SELECTOR SW.
2. MAIN DISTRIBUTION PANEL.
3. RECOGNITION LIGHTS CIRCUIT BREAKER
4. LANDING LIGHTS RELAYS
5. LANDING LIGHTS
6. FORMATION LIGHT - BLUE
7. STARBOARD WING LIGHT - GREEN
8. ANCHOR LIGHT - WHITE
9. RECOGNITION LIGHTS - RED, GREEN, AMBER & CLEAR
10. LANDING LIGHT FUSES
11. SECTION LIGHT - BLUE
12. TAIL LIGHT - WHITE
13. PORT WING LIGHT - RED
14. ANCHOR LIGHT SWITCH

Figure 35—Exterior Lights Diagram

Section II
Paragraph 18-19

AN 01-5MA-1

partment lights and extension light receptacles also are provided.

Exterior lights include position, formation, recognition, section, landing and anchor lights.

CAUTION

While the airplane is not in motion, if landing lights are operated more than five seconds, they will overheat and must be replaced.

Signal equipment includes a signal flare pistol, firing tube, and ammunition containers.

19. APPROACH AND LANDING.

See: Landing Check-Off List; Take-Off, Climb and Landing Chart and Stall Chart.

a. GENERAL.—Best landing approach speed depends on such factors as loading, altitude and position of landing gear or floats. Reference should be made to the Take-Off Climb and Landing Chart. *(See figure 64.)*

Pilot should check to see that his rate of descent is not too rapid, slowing it when necessary by increasing power and nosing up within safe IAS limits.

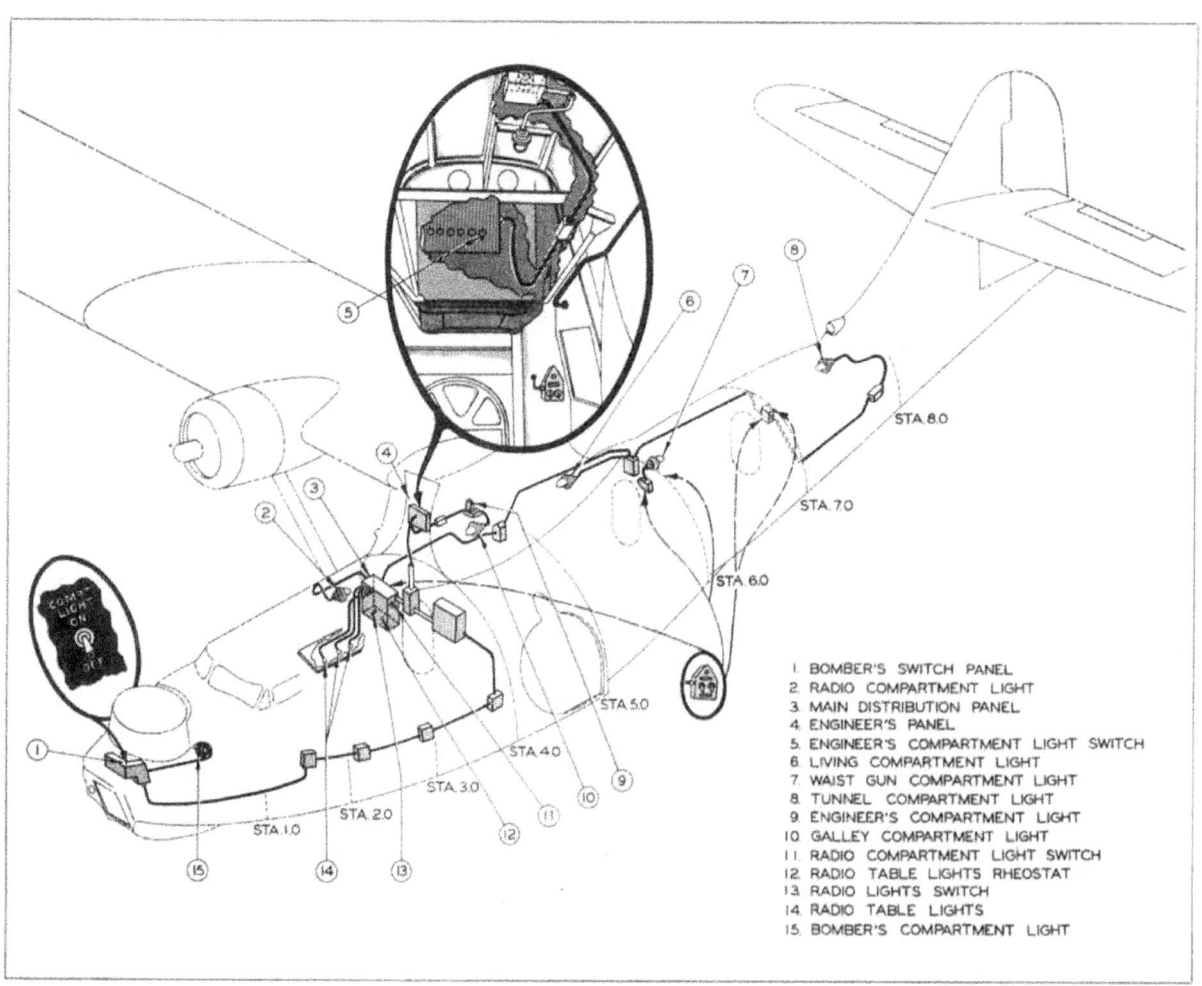

1. BOMBER'S SWITCH PANEL
2. RADIO COMPARTMENT LIGHT
3. MAIN DISTRIBUTION PANEL
4. ENGINEER'S PANEL
5. ENGINEER'S COMPARTMENT LIGHT SWITCH
6. LIVING COMPARTMENT LIGHT
7. WAIST GUN COMPARTMENT LIGHT
8. TUNNEL COMPARTMENT LIGHT
9. ENGINEER'S COMPARTMENT LIGHT
10. GALLEY COMPARTMENT LIGHT
11. RADIO COMPARTMENT LIGHT SWITCH
12. RADIO TABLE LIGHTS RHEOSTAT
13. RADIO LIGHTS SWITCH
14. RADIO TABLE LIGHTS
15. BOMBER'S COMPARTMENT LIGHT

Figure 36—Interior Lights Diagram

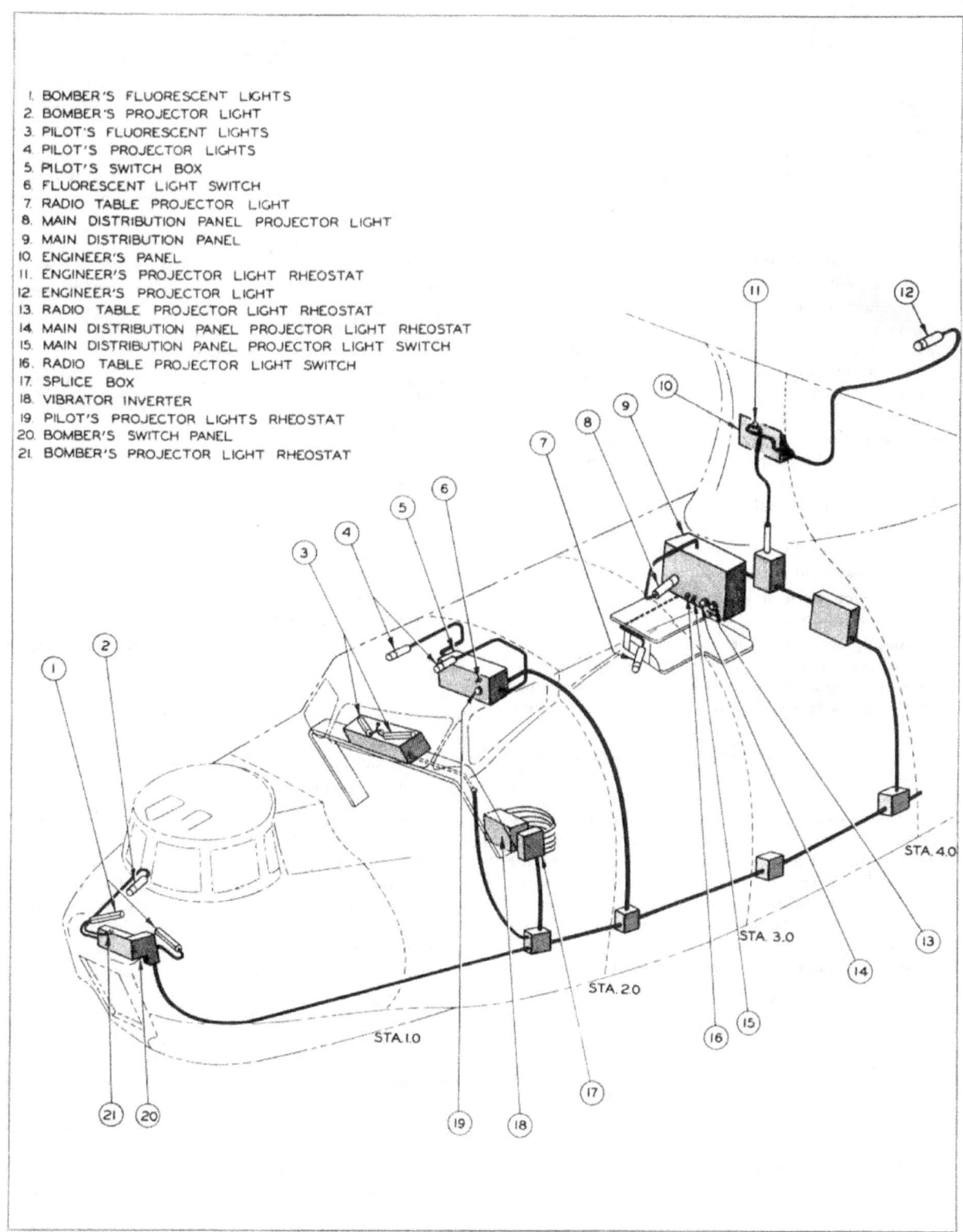

Figure 37—Fluorescent Lights Diagram

Sufficient speed above stalling speed should be maintained to insure maneuverability, particularly under bad visibility conditions. Set propeller for take-off rpm (low pitch).

When flying a heavy airplane, it should be especially remembered, that a body tends to maintain motion in a straight path. Therefore, if a steep glide is being made with accompanying high rate of descent, it takes time and a considerable force to flare out this rate of descent and change the motion to one parallel to the ground. It cannot reasonably be expected, with a rate of descent of over 500 ft/min, to start the flare 5 to 10 feet above the ground and make a soft landing.

It is desirable to have the cowl flaps closed during glides to prevent rapid cooling of the engines. A one-third open cowl flap position may be desirable, however, during the final approach, if there is a possibility of high power suddenly being needed to continue flight.

During long glides at part or closed throttle, with low air temperatures, occasional operation of the propeller and throttle controls is recommended in order to prevent congealing of the oil in the propeller cylinder. The pitch change introduces hot oil into the cylinder.

b. LANDING ON LAND.—The airplane shows no tendency to ground loop in a cross wind, but any drift should be taken out before making ground contact.

Maximum speed at which landing gear should be lowered is 120 knots.

Landing on smooth, prepared runways is permissible with gross weights up to 34,000 pounds. Lighter weights down to 26,000 pounds are recommended when landing on less favorable terrain under normal conditions.

Landings should ordinarily be made on the main wheels, with the nose wheel held off. After contact, the nose wheel should be held where it is until some speed is lost before easing it down to the runway. This procedure tends to keep the airplane in a high drag attitude as long as possible and to reduce the amount of braking required. However, the tail should not be held down until all control is lost, for this practice will result in dropping the nose violently. For the same reason, brakes should not be applied until all three wheels are on the ground, and the airplane has slowed as much as possible.

CAUTION

Care must be taken not to rock the airplane back on its keel during landing.

c. LANDING ON WATER.—When landing on rough water, a stall landing should be made.

WARNING

"Hot" landings on water are not recommended since excessive speed will peel off nose wheel doors and result in a serious accident.

Night landings, however, should be made with power to avoid a pancake landing in case altitude is misjudged. Night landings on water should be made with a slightly nose high attitude in the later stages of approach from an altitude of 200 feet on down, with an IAS of 76-83 knots. Power should be used to control rate of descent not exceeding 250 feet per minute.

Maximum speed at which floats should be lowered is 120 knots.

The airplane has a tendency to porpoise if landed at slow speeds. Minimum speeds should be observed. However, if the airplane is landed at an excessive speed, the nose will come up out of the water.

Maximum gross weight recommended for rough water landing is 27,300 pounds,—for smooth water, 34,500. At gross weights in excess of 30,000 pounds, the limiting weight which may be landed safely may depend on hydrodynamic considerations.

d. TAKE-OFF PROCEDURE IF LANDING NOT COMPLETED.—Take-off procedure, if landing is not completed, is as follows:

(1) Make sure propellers are in high rpm position.
(2) Advance throttle.
(3) Trim ship for take-off.
(4) Open cowl flaps.

e. PROCEDURE IF ENGINE FAILS ON LANDING.—If engine fails on landing, procedure recommended is as follows:

Take care not to lose air speed.

Trim rudder and aileron tabs. "HANDS-OFF" trim, if possible.

Place the propeller in the low rpm position, if possible.

Feather the useless propeller as soon as possible. If the prop cannot be feathered, it should be allowed to windmill in low rpm position.

Shut off fuel to useless engine, and shut off the fuel selector valve as soon as practical.

Place the propeller of the good engine in high rpm position, if power is needed to reach landing spot. (Do not exceed maximum permissible engine over-speed of 3,060 rpm for 30 seconds). Rapid settling of the airplane must be anticipated.

If the landing gear or floats have not been lowered at time of engine failure, considerable loss of altitude may be expected when they are lowered. If starboard engine fails, hydraulic system pump will be inoperative, and landing gear must be lowered by emergency methods requiring approximately three minutes. See "Emergency Operation of Landing Gear." If conditions permit, altitude should be attained, and a few landings simulated at safe altitude.

Floats can be lowered or raised in a maximum of 20 seconds.

No steep banks should be attempted, and banks should be made with the dead engine high, to avoid danger of spinning.

f. BEFORE LANDING—ON LAND.

PILOT

(1) Signal crew to prepare for landing.

(3) Lower landing gear.
(4) Check landing gear down and locked by moving indicator light switch to "INDICATOR LIGHTS."
(5) Check floats up.
(6) Trim ship for landing.
(7) Propellers—Set for 2450 to 2550 rpm.
(8) Signal engineer to shift to "AUTOMATIC RICH."

FLIGHT ENGINEER

(2) Check hatches and covers closed; bomber's window cover down.

(9) Mixture control — Set for "AUTOMATIC RICH."
(10) Cowl Flaps—Closed.
(11) Carburetor Air Control—"DIRECT" except when ice and sleet conditions require "ALTERNATE" setting.
(12) Open cowl flaps immediately after landing.

---

g. BEFORE LANDING—ON WATER.

PILOT

(1) Signal crew to prepare for landing and check wing anti-icer switches "OFF." Have navigator turn central heating unit off and signal engineer to turn off tail anti-icer. Check anti-icer switches off and signal engineer to turn off tail anti-icer. Instruct crew members to see that all hatches and openings are closed, bomber's window cover down.

(3) Signal "FLOATS DOWN."

(5) Check landing gear up and locked by moving indicator switch to "INDICATOR LIGHTS."
(6) Trim ship for landing.
(7) Propellers—Set for 2450 to 2550 rpm.
(8) Signal engineer to shift to "AUTOMATIC RICH."

FLIGHT ENGINEER

(2) Turn off tail anti-icer.

(4) Lower floats.

(9) Mixture Control — Set for "AUTOMATIC RICH."
(10) Cowl Flaps—Closed.
(11) Carburetor Air Control—"DIRECT" except when ice and sleet conditions require "ALTERNATE" setting.
(12) Second mechanic stand by sea anchor after landing.
(13) Open cowl flaps immediately after landing.

Section II
Paragraph 20-21

AN 01-5MA-1

20. STOPPING ENGINES.

PILOT

FLIGHT ENGINEER

a. Cowl flaps should be opened. Cylinder temperature should not exceed 200°C (392°F), before stopping, if practicable.

b. Throttles should be opened to 1000 rpm. (Cut switches if necessary when coming up to buoy or beach.)

c. Set propeller control in low pitch ("high rpm").

d. Signal engineer to stop engines.

e. Put mixture control in "IDLE CUT-OFF" position.

f. Cut switches after engines stop.

g. Signal "SECURE" after plane is beached or secured to buoy.

h. Instruct radio operator to secure lights and interphones.

i. Place landing gear indicator switch in center position.

j. Put on rudder locks and control yoke locks.

k. Install battens on control surfaces.

NOTE ON STOPPING AUXILIARY POWER UNIT

Except in an emergency, the auxiliary power unit should always be stopped by shutting off the fuel supply, rather than by grounding the magneto with the emergency stop button on the unit.

---

21. BEFORE LEAVING THE PILOT'S COMPARTMENT.

Check to see that cowl flaps are full open.

Check to see that ignition switches are both off.

Check to see that propellers are left in high rpm (low pitch).

Check with engineer to see that mixture control is in "IDLE CUT-OFF" and that fuel selector valves are off.

Lock the controls by the following procedure: First remove control lock from stowage and place aft end in socket located on forward face of bulkhead 2, just outboard of the pilot's seat. Move control yoke to neutral position so that pins at forward end of control lock fall into holes in the control yoke. These holes are located on either side of the pilot's control wheel on the top surface of the yoke.

To release rudder lock pull latch which is located approximately at the center of the rudder lock handle and move handle aft until it is approximately adjacent to the side of the airplane. The rudder lock is located to the left of the pilot, against the side of the airplane and is marked "RUDDER LOCK." *(See figure 1.)*

Check to see that automatic pilot is off.

If on land, set parking brakes after waiting for brakes to cool to normal temperature. Parking brakes are located to the right of the co-pilot. To set the brake, press down brake pedals and pull handle down.

Turn out lights.

★   ★   ★

SECTION III
FLIGHT OPERATING DATA

1. SPECIFIC ENGINE FLIGHT CHART. *(Fig. 38.)*
(Also see figure 68.)

The definitions of the engine power ratings shown on the chart are as follows:

a. TAKE-OFF.—Maximum recommended for take-off under the specified time limit.

b. MILITARY RATING.—This is the maximum power permitted with less regard for long life of the engine than for immediate tactical needs. Military rating, comparable to Take-Off Power with manifold pressures modified to suit altitude conditions, may be used for five minutes.

c. NORMAL RATING (Maximum Continuous.)—This is frequently referred to as either "Normal Maximum Rating" or "Maximum-Except Take-Off Power." This is the maximum power at which an engine may be operated continuously for emergency (such as single engine) or high performance operation in climb or level flight. This rating is considered 100 per cent power and speed as a basis from which other operating conditions are calculated.

d. MAXIMUM CRUISE RATING.—This rating limits both the maximum power and maximum rpm permissible for continuous operation with the mixture control in "AUTOMATIC LEAN." The Specific Engine Flight Chart shows the maximum rpm at which the maximum cruising bmep may be maintained.

e. MINIMUM SPECIFIC CONSUMPTION.—Under most conditions of cruising operation, it is neither necessary nor desirable to use the maximum cruising power available from the engine. In such instances maximum engine efficiency and, as a rule, propeller efficiency is attained by maintaining the maximum permissible cruising torque or brake mean effective pressure as set forth on the bmep Cruising Chart. *(See figure 66.)* The Specific Engine Flight Chart shows the maximum rpm and a representative low rpm at which the maximum cruising bmep may be maintained. Other power and speed combinations may be selected from the operating curve and lower values may be extrapolated.

2. AIR SPEED LIMITATIONS.
Note
The flight limitations and restrictions on this airplane are subject to change and the latest service instructions and technical orders must be consulted.

a. MAXIMUM SPEEDS.—Restricted speeds for gross weights in excess of 26,000 pounds are given in the table below. The restricted speed for any load in extremely rough air is 110 knots.

Gross Weight (Pounds)	Permissible Speed (Knots—Indicated)
26,000	190
28,000	175
30,000	165
32,000	155
34,000	145
36,000	125

b. In addition to the above restrictions on speed, increasing care is considered essential at these increased gross weights in methods of operation which cannot be expressed in figures. For example, turns should be more moderate and all control movements should be smoother.

c. Floats should not be lowered at indicated speeds greater than 120 knots.

d. Landing gear should not be lowered at speeds greater than 120 knots.

e. MINIMUM SPEEDS.—(Refer to Section II, Par. 14 for stalling speeds.) Do not operate on automatic pilot at indicated air speeds of less than 85 knots.

3. AIR SPEED CALIBRATION CHART.
(See figure 39.)

4. BALANCE COMPUTER DESIGNATION.
The balance computer used on this airplane is known as the "Load Adjuster."

Section III

AN 01-5MA-1

SPECIFIC ENGINE FLIGHT CHART

AIRPLANE MODELS: PBY-5A

ENGINE MODELS: PRATT & WHITNEY R-1830-92

CONDITION	FUEL PRESSURE (LB./SQ. IN.)	OIL PRESSURE (LB./SQ. IN.)	OIL TEMP. °C	OIL TEMP. °F	CYLINDER TEMP. °C	CYLINDER TEMP. °F
DESIRED	17	85	65	149		
MAXIMUM	18	100	100	212		
MINIMUM	16	65	40	104		
IDLING	11	15	40	104		

MAX. PERMISSIBLE DIVING RPM: 3060 (30 SECONDS DURATION ONLY)

CONDITION	ALLOWABLE OIL CONSUMPTION
NORMAL RATED (MAX. CONT.)	.... U.S.QT./HR .... IMP.PT/HR
MAX. CRUISE	.... U.S.QT./HR .... IMP.PT/HR
MIN. SPECIFIC	.... U.S.QT./HR .... IMP.PT/HR

OIL GRADE: 1120, AN-V.V.-O.446

SUPERCHARGER TYPE: SINGLE STAGE - SINGLE SPEED BLOWER TYPE **FUEL GRADE**: 100/130, AN-F-28

OPERATING CONDITION	RPM	MANIFOLD PRESSURE (BOOST)	HORSE-POWER	CRITICAL ALTITUDE WITH RAM	CRITICAL ALTITUDE NO RAM	BLOWER	USE LOW BLOWER BELOW:	MIXTURE CONTROL POSITION	FUEL FLOW (GAL./HR./ENG.) U.S.	FUEL FLOW IMP.	MAXIMUM CYL. TEMP. °C	MAXIMUM CYL. TEMP. °F	MAXIMUM DURATION (MINUTES)
TAKE-OFF	2700	48	1200	S.L.	S.L.			AR	150	118	260	500	5
WAR EMERGENCY													
MILITARY	2700	45**	1200	S.L. TO 4800	4800			AR	150	118	260	500	5
NORMAL RATED (MAX. CONT.)	2550	39.5	1050	S.L. TO 7500	7000			AR	114	95	260 / 232	500 / 450	60 CONTINUOUS
MAXIMUM CRUISE	2170	30.5	700	S.L. TO 15,000	10200			AL	60	50	232	450	CONTIN-UOUS
MINIMUM SPECIFIC CONSUMPTION	1750*	31*	560	S.L.	6600			AL	37	31	232	450	CONTIN-UOUS

REMARKS:
* This representative power setting will give best engine economy at 140 psi bmep, but not necessarily best miles per gallon.

** Limit at 4800 feet. Reduce manifold pressure proportionately with increasing altitude from 48" Hg. at S.L. to 45" Hg. at 4800 feet. Manifold pressures listed are limits at no-ram critical altitudes.

FORM ASC-512A

Figure 38—Specific Engine Flight Chart

62

Section III
AN 01-5MA-1

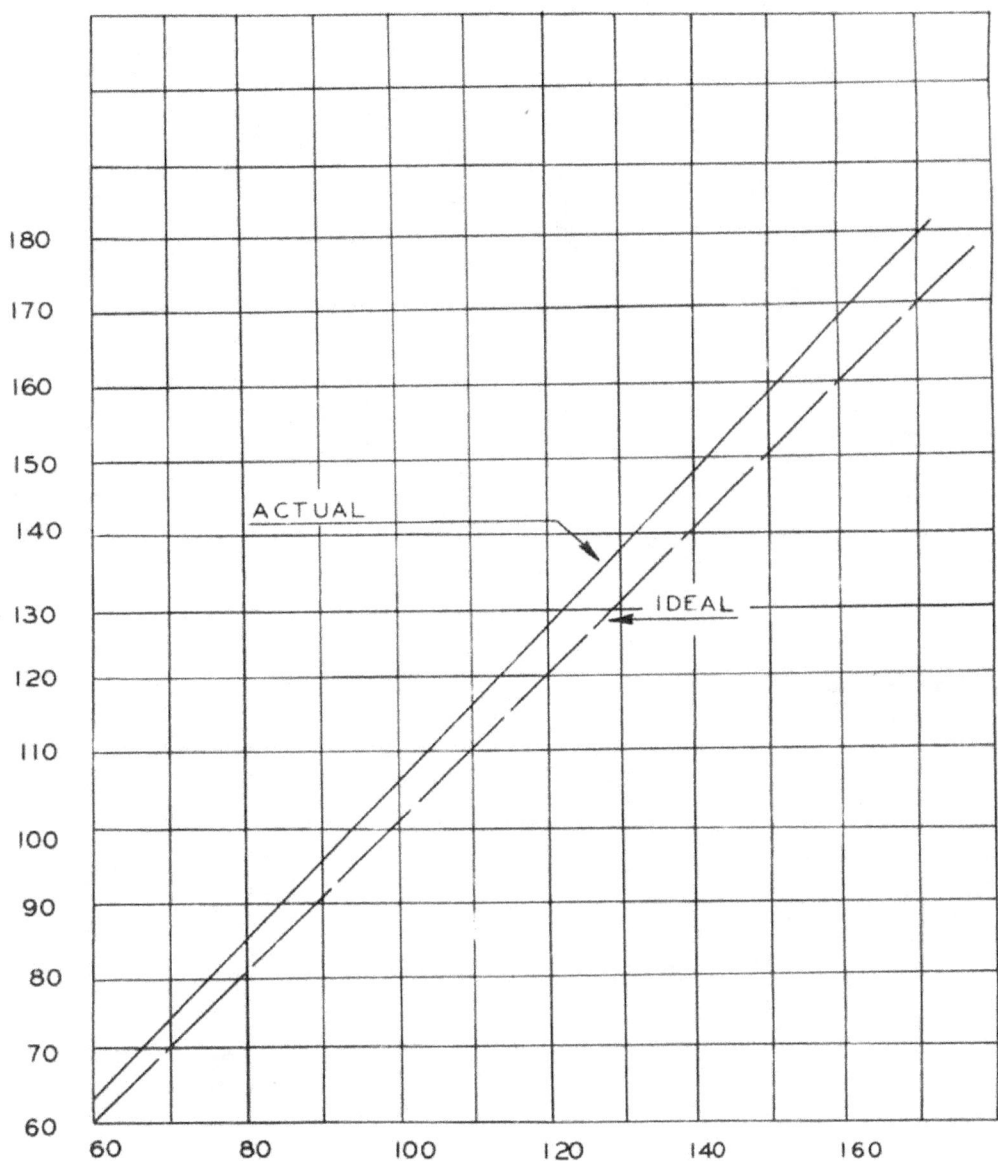

AIR SPEED INDICATOR READING ** KNOTS

Figure 39—Air Speed Correction Chart

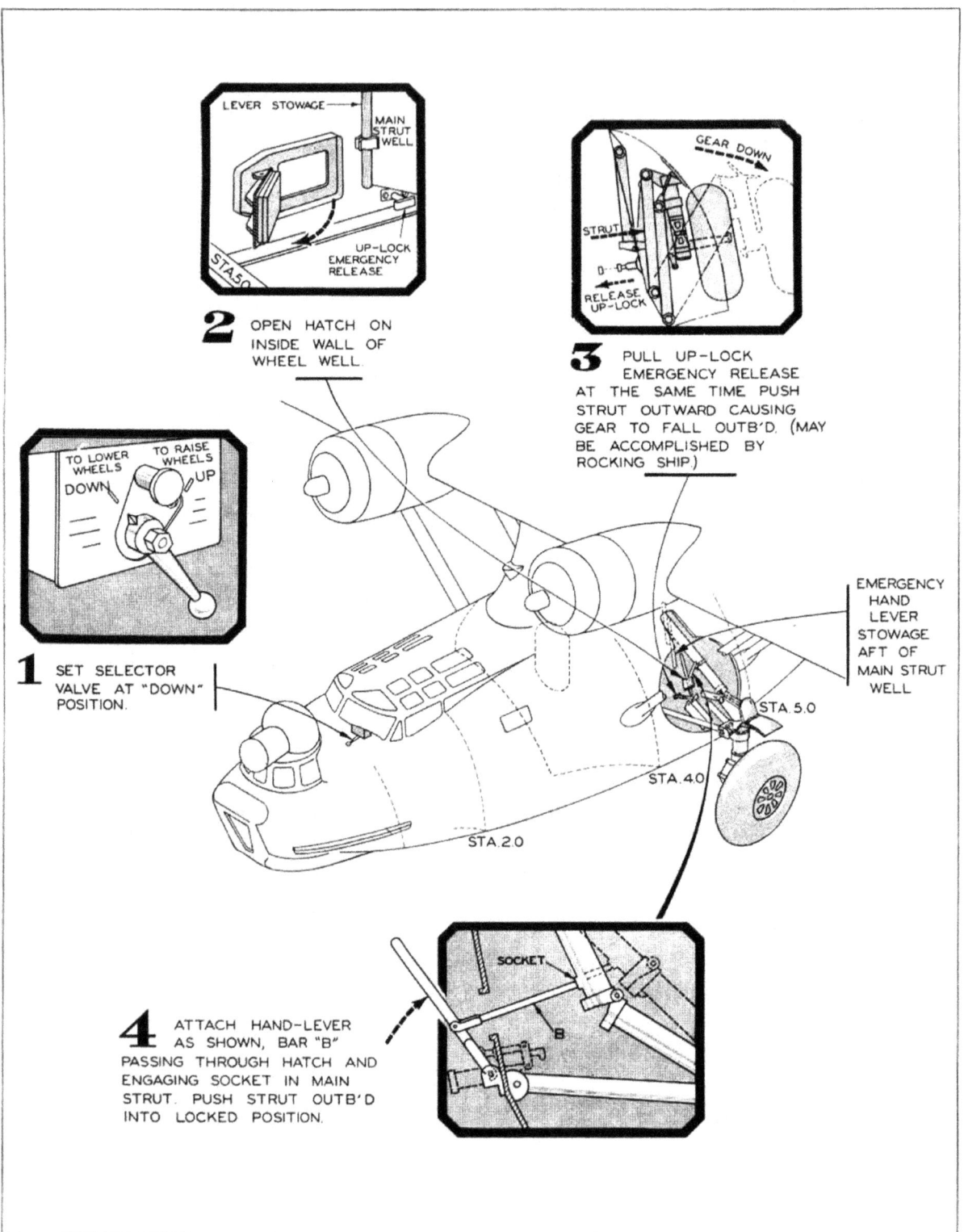

Figure 40—Emergency Lowering of Main Landing Gear

AN 01-5MA-1

Section IV
Paragraph 1

SECTION IV
EMERGENCY OPERATION

1. EMERGENCY OPERATION OF LANDING GEAR.

(See figures 40, 41 and 44.)

a. If gear fails to lower when handle is pushed down, check hydraulic pressure gage. If gage shows above 1000 lbs pressure, return handle to up position and repeat attempt to lower gear. If gear does not lower on second attempt, leave gear handle locked in down position and:

b. Release the main wheel up locks by pulling out the "Tee" handles at the main wheel wells and turning handles ¼ turn.

c. Work gear down by rocking the airplane approximately 14° to each side.

d. Use the emergency "DOWN-LATCH" lever to straighten out the main support struts and latch the gear in the down position. To do this, first insert emergency "DOWN-LATCH" lever through access door provided in side of wheel well, and engage the handle end of the lever over the bolt provided on the auxiliary keel. With handle end of lever supported by the bolt, guide the outboard end of the lever into the strut socket located just above the pivot point in the strut.

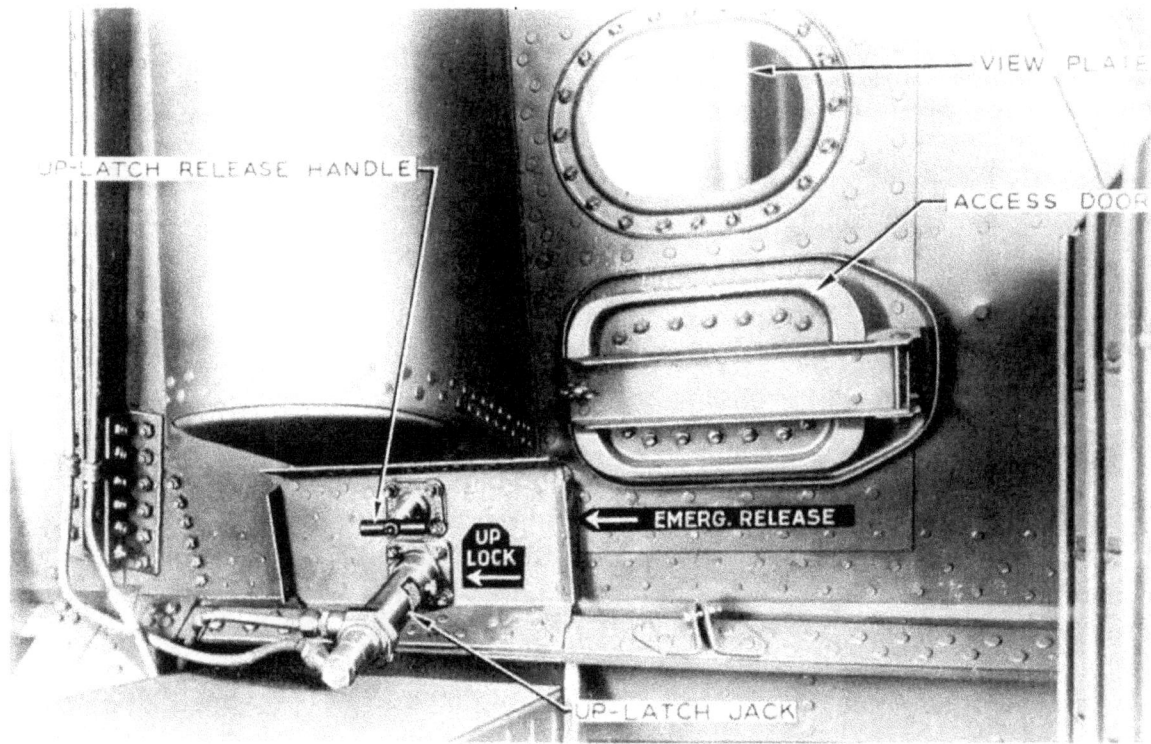

Figure 41—Emergency Up-Latch Release Handle and Access Door

Section IV
Paragraph 1-2

AN 01-5MA-1

e. Push firmly on the lever to straighten out the strut and the gear will latch down. Repeat same operation for gear on opposite side.

f. Unlock nose wheel doors by pushing door lock handle aft, (located on the starboard side, forward of bulkhead 1) thus releasing the door lock pins.

g. Insert hydraulic hand pump handle or emergency "DOWN-LATCH" lever handle in the aft end of the starboard door torque tube, (located aft of bulkhead 2) and push inboard, (counterclockwise) rotating the torque tube and thus opening the nose wheel well doors.

Note

In airplanes where the radar antennae have been installed, it will not be possible to use the emergency "DOWN-LATCH" lever for emergency manual operation of the nose wheel well doors. However, the hydraulic hand pump handle may be substituted for this purpose.

h. Lock torque tube in "DOORS OPEN" position by swinging locking link inboard over the lug on the torque tube end fitting. Insert locking pin and retain with safety pin.

i. Remove aft nose wheel cover plug and insert emergency lever through the hole. Strike the end of the up-latch sharply to unlatch the nose gear.

j. Attach the emergency lever to the torque tube between the packing nut and the jack fitting, so that the ratchet pawl fits into the teeth of the jack fitting. Using the lever as a ratchet, force the gear into the down position. To lock, use a slow, heavy push.

k. Remove the forward plug of the wheel well cover to examine the down-latch, and use emergency "DOWN-LATCH" lever to determine if the down-latch is locked. If it is locked, the red collar on the lever will not extend above the hole in the cover, and the oleo strut will be vertical and against the down bumper.

CAUTION

Before operating gear again, be sure to release the emergency door lockpin.

If the landing gear failure is due to failure of starboard engine or engine-driven hydraulic pump, and not to loss of fluid caused by leaking reservoir or lines, the gear may be lowered with pressure supplied by the hand pump. Latch control handle in "DOWN" position before operating pump. Be sure to check "gear down and latched" with indicator lights. To raise gear, latch control handle in "UP" position and operate hand pump as described above.

2. EMERGENCY OPERATION OF FLOATS.

(See figures 42 and 43.)

a. TO LOWER FLOATS.

(1) Remove hand crank from stowage on starboard side of bulkhead below engineer's seat.

(2) Engage crank in socket marked "FAST," in center of bulkhead below engineer's seat, and crank counterclockwise.

b. TO RAISE FLOATS.—Insert crank in socket marked "FAST" and turn clockwise until load gets too

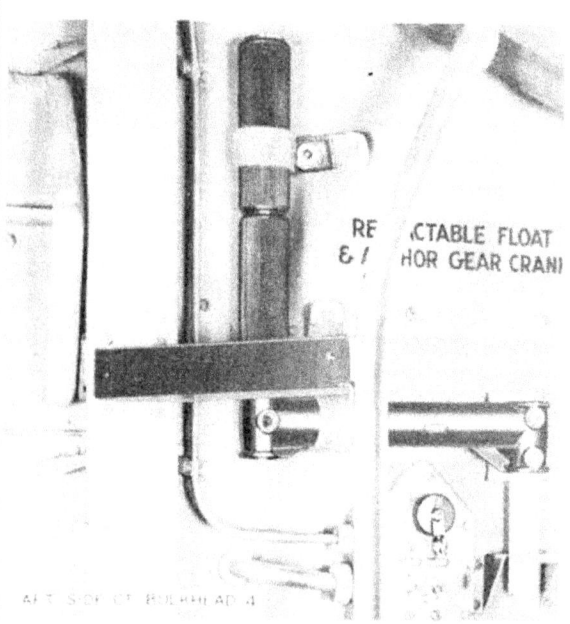

Figure 42—Float Crank in Stowed Position

Figure 43—Float Crank Ready to Operate

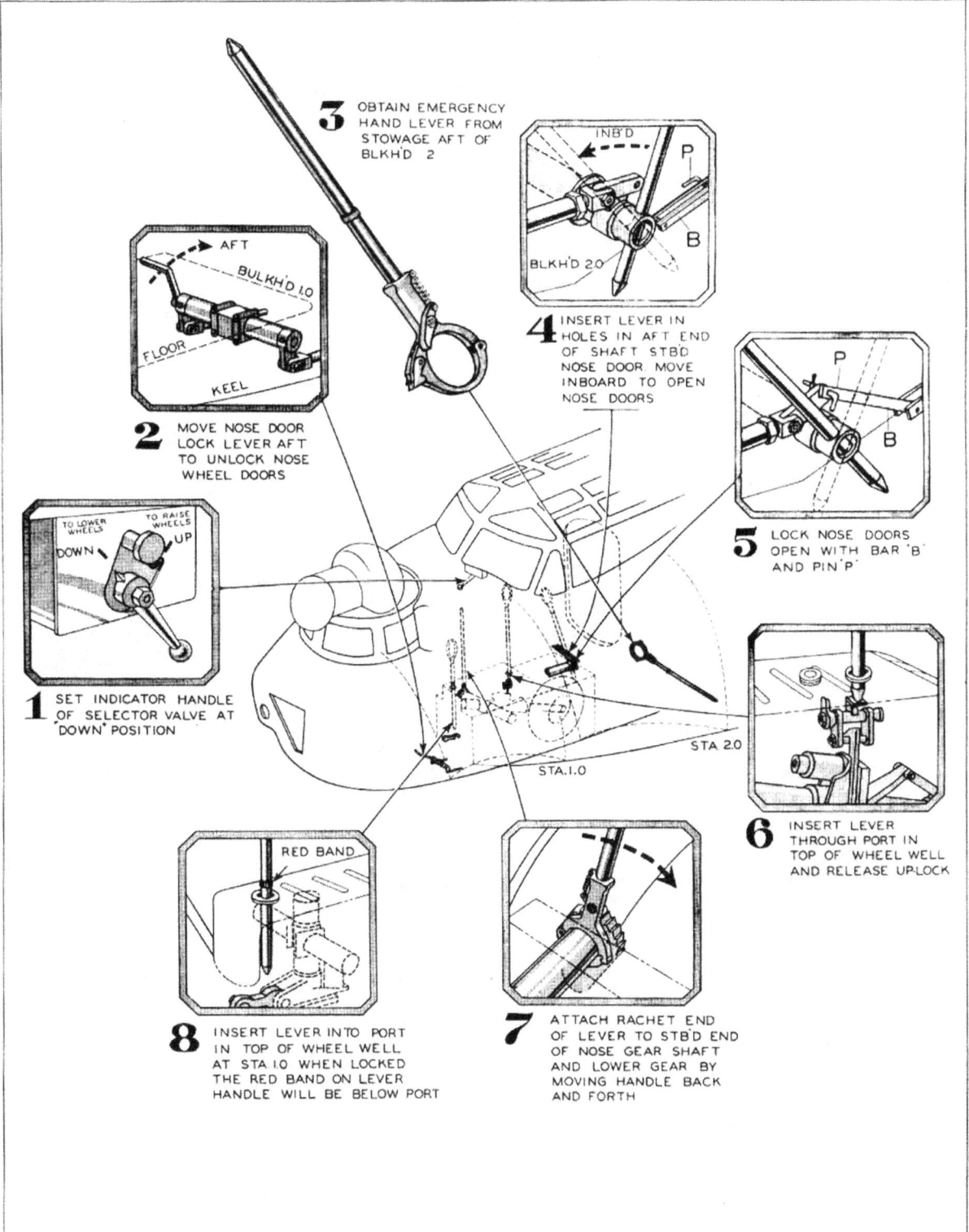

Figure 44—Emergency Lowering of Nose Gear

Section IV
Paragraph 2-3-4-5   AN 01-5MA-1

heavy to operate easily. To raise floats remainder of the distance, move crank to "SLOW" socket, and continue to turn clockwise until floats are latched in up position.

3. EMERGENCY TAKE-OFF.

If oil was diluted when engines were last stopped, take-off may be made as soon as pressure is steady at around 65 to 75 pounds.

If oil was not diluted, the oil dilution valve may be opened intermittently, after starting engines at intervals of a few seconds for a period of about 15 seconds, or until oil pressure is steady.

Be sure propellers are in highest rpm (full low pitch) position.

Leave cowl flaps open. Closing cowl flaps will not assist warm-up, and will damage engine.

Proceed with normal take-off.

4. ENGINE FAILURE DURING TAKE-OFF.

In case of engine failure at a low air speed and a low altitude, the pilot must immediately choose between either throttling the remaining engine and landing straight ahead, if the ground or water is suitable, or retracting landing gear or floats, carefully building up speed, and continuing in flight until a safe landing can be effected.

If decision is made to land on ground ahead, less damage will probably be done if the landing gear is retracted.

If the landing is to be made on good terrain, but in limited space, the airplane should be stalled in, then brought promptly to the three-point attitude and brakes applied. Landings of this type can be made successfully, if tires and brakes are in good condition.

If continued flight is undertaken, all maneuvers should be made as gently as possible, to avoid an attitude from which recovery is impossible.

For minimum and best air speed, see Stalling Speed Chart. The pilot must overcome any tendency to pull nose up before sufficient air speed has been obtained.

Where it is necessary to obtain altitude immediately, landing gear or floats should be retracted. However, the hydraulic pump is located on the starboard engine, so failure of that engine will make retraction of the landing gear impossible except by emergency methods requiring approximately five minutes. See "Emergency Operation of Landing Gear." Floats are controlled electrically, so failure of an engine will not affect their operation. Time required to retract the floats is 20 seconds.

The airplane must be trimmed (rudder tab first, aileron tab second) for as good a "hands off" condition as possible.

Banks must be made with the dead engine high, and only shallow banks should be attempted.

Feather the useless propeller to reduce the drag. If propeller cannot be feathered, place it in low rpm position to reduce vibration. Sufficient air speed will cause the propeller to windmill and turn the dead engine over fast enough to pump oil for the propeller pitch changing mechanism.

Leave propeller of the useful engine in the high rpm position to give maximum engine power output. Shut off the fuel to the useless engine with the fuel selector valve as soon as practicable. The use of more than rated power at any altitude must be kept to a minimum to avoid overheating and detonation which will result in damage too, if not complete failure of, the remaining engine. The use of rich mixture will help slightly to keep engine cylinder temperatures down.

When landing, rapid settling of the airplane must be anticipated, particularly at the time landing gear or floats are lowered. Before landing is attempted, pilot should gain all the altitude possible, and where practical, simulate landing procedure by lowering wheels or floats and reducing power. Lowering of the wheels by use of the emergency hand pump will require approximately three minutes. See "Emergency Operation of Landing Gear."

5. ENGINE FAILURE DURING LANDING.

If engine fails on landing, procedure recommended is as follows:

Take care not to lose air speed.

Trim rudder and aileron tabs. "HANDS-OFF" trim, if possible.

Place the propeller in the low rpm position, if possible.

Feather the useless propeller as soon as possible. If prop cannot be feathered, it should be allowed to windmill in low rpm position.

Shut off fuel to useless engine, and shut off the fuel selector valve as soon as practical.

Place the propeller of the good engine in high rpm position, if power is needed to reach landing spot. (Do not exceed maximum permissible engine overspeed of 3,060 rpm for 30 seconds). Rapid settling of the airplane must be anticipated.

If the landing gear or floats have not been lowered at time of engine failure, considerable loss of altitude may be expected when they are lowered. If starboard engine fails, hydraulic system pump will be inoperative, and landing gear must be lowered by emergency methods requiring approximately three minutes. See "Emergency Operation of Landing Gear." If conditions permit, altitude should be attained, and a few landings simulated at safe altitude.

Floats can be lowered or raised in a maximum of 20 seconds.

No steep banks should be attempted, and banks should be made with the dead engines high, to avoid danger of spinning.

Section IV

AN 01-5MA-1

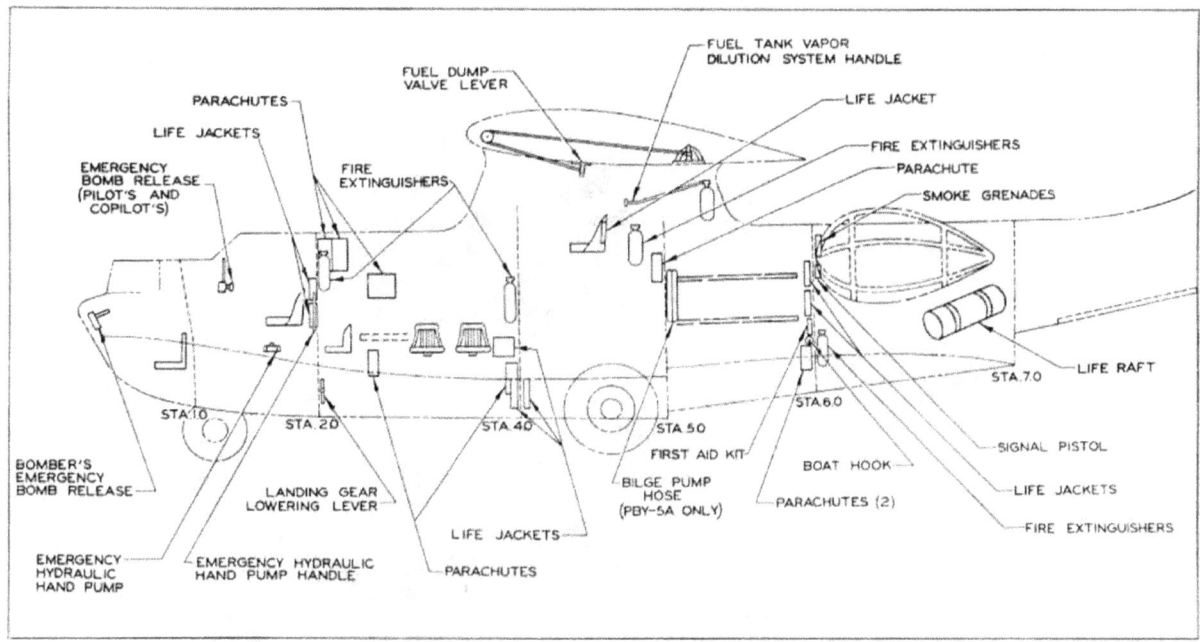

Emergency Equipment Locations

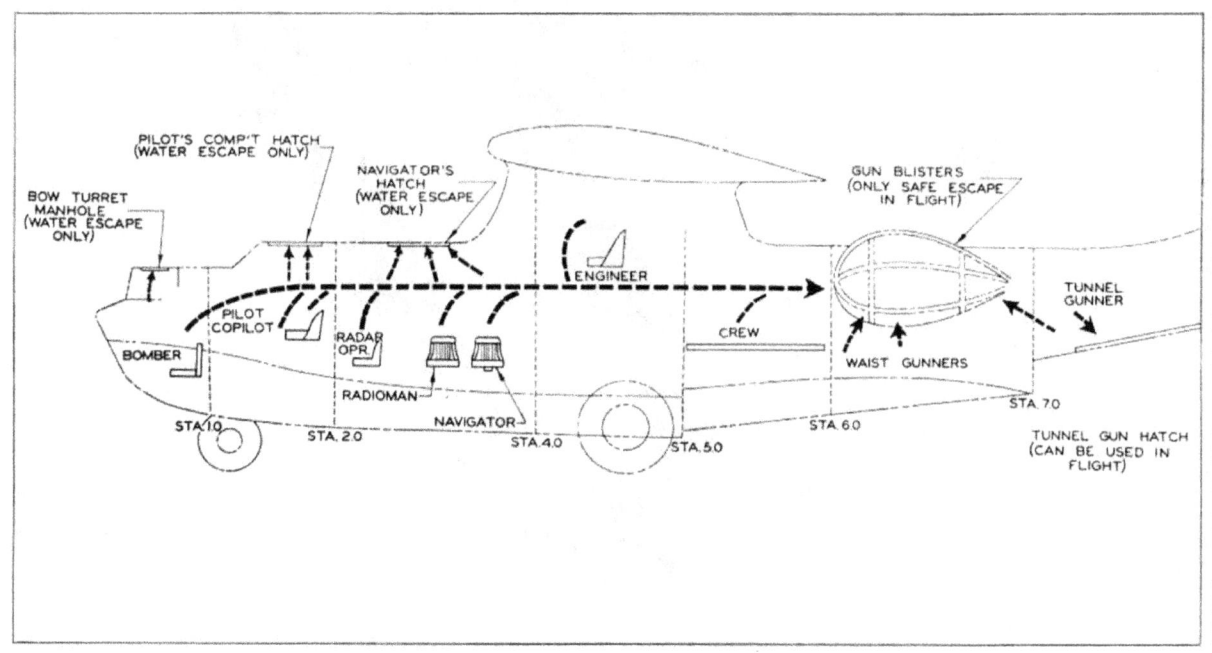

Emergency Escape Routes

Figure 45—Emergency Equipment and Escape Routes

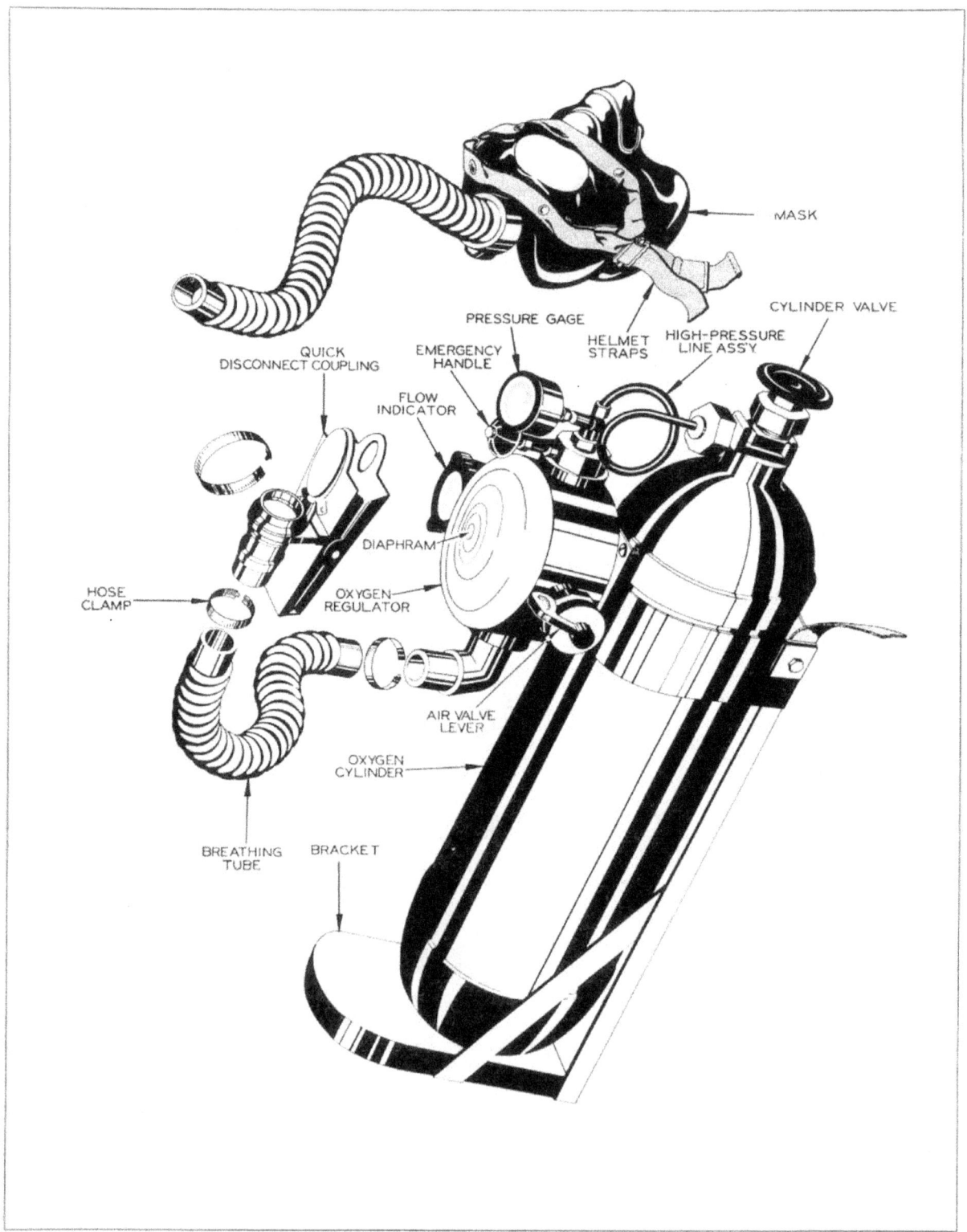

Figure 46—Portable Oxygen Equipment

SECTION V
OPERATIONAL EQUIPMENT

1. REMOTE COMPARTMENTS.

The compartments containing operating equipment not accessible to the pilot and co-pilot have been described in Section 1 under the following paragraphs:

2, *b*. Engineer's Compartment.

2, *c*. Controls in Radio Operator-Navigator's Compartment.

2, *d*. Crew's Quarters.

2, *e*. Waist Gun Compartment.

2, *f*. Tail Compartment.

The Bow Gunner-Bomber's compartment equipment will be discussed in paragraph 4 of this section under Armament.

2. OPERATION OF OXYGEN EQUIPMENT.

(See figure 46.)

By means of service action, this airplane will carry two portable individual supply type diluter-demand oxygen units which have their own integral supply system, oxygen regulators and flow indicators. Mountings for these units are placed at the pilot's, co-pilot's and engineer's stations. The units may be carried to the various parts of the airplane as required.

CHECK LIST

This check list is to be used prior to take-off whenever there may be a possibility of flight to oxygen altitudes.

a. Close emergency valve.

b. Open cylinder valve, allowing at least 10 seconds for pressure in line to equalize. Pressure gage should read 1800 ± 50 pounds per square inch if the cylinder is fully charged.

c. Close cylinder valve after a few minutes, observing pressure gage, and simultaneously open cylinder valve. If gage pointer jumps, leakage is indicated.

d. If leakage is indicated, test further. Open cylinder valve, carefully noting pressure gage reading, then close cylinder valve. If gage pointer drops more than 100 pounds per square inch in five minutes, there is excessive leakage and the unit must be repaired prior to use.

e. Check mask fit by placing thumb over end of mask tube and inhale lightly. If there is no leakage, mask will adhere tightly to face, due to suction created. If mask leaks, tighten mask suspension straps and adjust nose wire.

WARNING
Do not use mask that leaks.

f. Couple mask securely to breathing tube by means of quick-disconnect coupling.

CAUTION
Mating parts of coupling must be fully engaged, and not "cocked."

g. Open cylinder valve. Depress diaphragm knob through hole in center of regulator case, and feel flow of oxygen into the mask; then close diaphragm knob. Breathe several times, observing oxygen flow indicator for "blink", verifying the positive flow of oxygen.

Note
Since the amount of added oxygen is very small at sea level, the oxygen flow indicator may not operate while the plane is on the ground. In this case, turn air-valve to "OFF" or to "ONE-HUNDRED PER CENT OXYGEN", and test again. If oxygen flow indicator operation is now satisfactory, re-set air-valve to "ON" or "NORMAL OXYGEN", in which setting adequate oxygen flow and "blinker" operation will be assured at oxygen use altitudes.

h. Check emergency valve by turning counterclockwise slowly until oxygen flows vigorously into mask, then close emergency valve.

OPERATING INSTRUCTIONS

Oxygen shall be used at all flights above 10,000 feet and on night flights above 5,000 feet (except by personnel whose keenness of night vision is not essential). On flights of more than four hours between 8,000 and 10,000 feet, oxygen should be used at least 15 minutes out of each hour.

a. Open oxygen cylinder valve. Pressure gage should read 1,800 ± 50 pounds per square inch if cylinder is fully charged.

CAUTION

If cylinder is not fully charged, replace with a new cylinder and re-check.

b. Set regulator air-valve to "ON" or "NORMAL OXYGEN" except when presence of excessive carbon monoxide is suspected—then set to "OFF" or "100 PERCENT OXYGEN."

c. Put on oxygen mask and couple securely to breathing tube by means of quick-disconnect coupling.

CAUTION

Be sure that quick-disconnect coupling is fully engaged.

d. Check mask fit as outlined in "Check List."

CAUTION

Never check mask fit by squeezing mask tube while Emergency Valve is "ON."

e. Depress diaphragm knob through hole in center of regulator case and feel flow of oxygen into mask; then release diaphragm knob. Breathe several times, observing oxygen flow indicator (if installed) for "blink," which verifies the positive flow of oxygen.

Note

Do not use oxygen supply below 300 pounds per square inch, except in an emergency.

f. Upon completion of oxygen usage, close cylinder valve.

WARNING

Use emergency valve only if regulator becomes inoperative or anoxia is suspected.

3. OPERATION OF COMMUNICATIONS EQUIPMENT.

a. GENERAL PLAN OF RADIO AND INTERCOMMUNICATING SYSTEM. *(See figure 48.)*—Radio equipment on this airplane originally consisted of a GO-9 transmitter and RU-19 receiver for long range communications; an ATB transmitter, and two ARB receivers for intrasquadron communications; a DW-1 direction finder; a ZA blind landing set; ZB-3 equipment; and an LM-10 frequency meter. In addition, provisions were made for the following radar equipment: ABA, ABK, ABD, ASV, and ASB.

By order of BuAer Service Changes part of this equipment is being replaced with a newer type. The equipment to be removed consists of the ZA blind landing set, the ZB-3 equipment, and the ABK, ABD, ASV, and ASB radar equipment. New equipment being installed consists of AN/APX-2 IFF equipment and AN/APS-3 radar.

Interphone equipment *(See figure 47)* is Type RL-24c, with 11 plug-in jack boxes at various crew stations throughout the airplane. The main control box for the interphone system is on the radio operator's table. A selector switch panel is located in the top center of bulkhead 2, aft of the pilot's and co-pilot's seats.

Pilot's ATB selector switch box is on the starboard side of bulkhead 2, back of the co-pilot's seat. Pilot's ARB selector switch box and remote tuning head are on the port side of bulkhead 2, back of the pilot's seat.

The GO-9 transmitting equipment is installed immediately forward of the radio operator's table and consists of three cabinets. The outboard cabinet contains the high frequency equipment, the center cabinet contains the power controls and instruments, and the inboard cabinet contains the intermediate frequency equipment.

The trailing antenna and reel, used with the GO-9 equipment are mounted in a bracket near the forward end of the radio operator's table.

The RU-19 receiver is on the forward end of the shelf over the radio operator's table. The radio operator's switch box is under the shelf over the radio operator's table. A second RU-19 switch box and a remote tuner are in the pilot's compartment.

The RU-19 junction box is near the forward end of the shelf over the radio operator's table and the RU-19 dynamotor is on the floor under the center of the radio operator's table.

Four spare RU-19 tuning coils are stowed on the ceiling of the compartment over the radio operator's table. Four more coils are stowed near the floor on the starboard side of bulkhead 4.

The LM-10 frequency meter is on the shelf over the radio operator's table.

The key for all transmitters is on the radio operator's table.

The ATB transmitter is on a shelf above the GO-9 transmitter. The ATB metering kit is on top of the ATB transmitter. The ATB spare tuning unit is near the ceiling of the radio operator-navigator's compartment, ahead of the ARB receiver.

The pilot's ARB receiver is on the shelf over the GO-9 equipment. Pilot's ARB controls are back of his seat, as previously stated.

Radio operator's ARB receiver is on the aft end of the shelf over the radio operator's table. Radio operator's ARB control switch box is on the underside of shelf over radio operator's table.

The DW-1 direction finder loop coupler unit is slightly forward of bulkhead 4 over the bulkhead door. The azimuth scale is above the coupler on the loop antenna shaft.

The output meter for the DW-1 direction finder is slightly outboard of the DW-1 loop coupler unit.

In addition to the above equipment, controls for radar equipment and miscellaneous power boxes, junction boxes and coils are located in the vicinity of the radio operator's table. The radio d-c power switch is on the forward face of bulkhead 4, under the main power distribution panel. The a-c power box is higher up on the same bulkhead, outboard of the main distribution panel.

b. OPERATION OF INTERPHONE SYSTEM.—Plug-in jack boxes with individual volume control knobs are located at 11 places throughout the airplane. These 11 places include all the regular crew operating stations. The pilot's, co-pilot's, radio operator's and navigator's station boxes allow the headphones and microphones to be connected to the ATB/ARB intrasquadron equipment by means of the pilot's and radio operator's control switches.

The pilot's control switches provide for the following combinations of hookups between pilots and radio operator, with the navigator able to plug into whichever lines are active.

Position 1. Co-pilot's microphone and one head phone connected to interphone system. Co-pilot's second headphone connected to intrasquadron receiver. Pilot's microphone and both headphones connected to intrasquadron set (receiver and transmitter).

Position 2. Co-pilot's microphone and both headphones connected to the intrasquadron set. Pilot's microphone and one headphone connected to the interphone system. Pilot's second headphone connected to the intrasquadron receiver.

Position 3. Co-pilot's microphone and one head phone connected to the interphone system. Co-pilot's second headphone connected to the intrasquadron receiver. Identical hookup for pilot.

Position 4. Both head sets and microphones connected to the interphone system only.

In addition to the selector switches, the pilot's interphone control box has a toggle switch for cutting the radio operator's ARB receiver in or out, two volume control knobs, and a recall light button for signalling the radio operator when the radio operator's head set is not connected to the interphone circuit.

The radio operator's interphone control box has a selector knob with six marked positions, which allow the radio operator to choose the following hookups:

Position 1. One headphone on receiver "A" (RU-19 receiver) and one headphone on receiver "B" (radio operator's ARB receiver) and interphone.

Position 2. One headphone on receiver "A" and one headphone on the interphone.

Position 3. One headphone on receiver "B" and one headphone on the interphone.

Position 4. Both headphones on the interphone.

Position 5. Both headphones on receiver "A."

Position 6. Both headphones on receiver "B."

In addition to the selector knob the control box has a power switch, an interphone "ON-OFF" switch, a pilot's recall light, and a volume control knob.

c. OPERATION OF ATB TRANSMITTER.

(1) TO TURN THE TRANSMITTER ON.—The pilot moves his selector switch from "OFF" position to "CHAN. 1" or "CHAN. 2" depending on operating frequency desired. (For explanation of channels, see (5) OPERATION FREQUENCIES.) The radio operator places the "TUNE-OPERATE" switch on the transmitter in the "OPERATE" position.

(2) TO CONNECT THE TRANSMITTER FOR VOICE TRANSMISSION.—The pilot moves the "VOICE-CODE" switch on his control box to "VOICE" position. He connects his microphone lead to the "MIC" jack at the bottom of the control box. The microphone switch must be pressed (closed) during the periods that actual voice transmission is desired.

(3) TO CONNECT THE TRANSMITTER FOR TONE (MODULATED CONTINUOUS WAVE.)—The pilot moves the "VOICE-CODE" switch to "CODE" position. The radio operator sets the "MCW-CW" switch on the transmitter in "MCW" position. The MCW code signals may then be transmitted by the key on the pilot's control box or by a key externally connected to the "KEY" jack at the transmitter.

(4) TO CONNECT THE TRANSMITTER FOR CW (CODE) TRANSMISSION.—The radio operator sets the "MCW-CW" switch on the transmitter to the "CW" position. The pilot sets the "VOICE-CODE" switch on his control box to "CODE" position. "CW" signals may then be sent either by use of the key on the pilot's control box, or by a key plugged in at the "KEY" jack on the transmitter.

(5) OPERATING FREQUENCIES.—Three tuning units are provided with the transmitter. Two of the units may be tuned to any frequency between 3.0 and 9.05 megacycles. The other (low frequency) between 2.3 and 4.2 megacycles. Two locations are provided in the transmitter for tuning units, known as channel 1 and channel 2. Any tuning unit may be installed in either channel. For purposes of switching, the location toward the left of the transmitter front panel is channel 1 and the location at the right is channel 2. The radio operator sets up the tuning combinations at the transmitter, and the pilot selects either channel 1 or channel 2 by means of the channel selector switch on his control box.

(6) TO TURN THE TRANSMITTER OFF.—Move the channel selector switch on the pilot's control box to "OFF."

Section V

AN 01-5MA-1

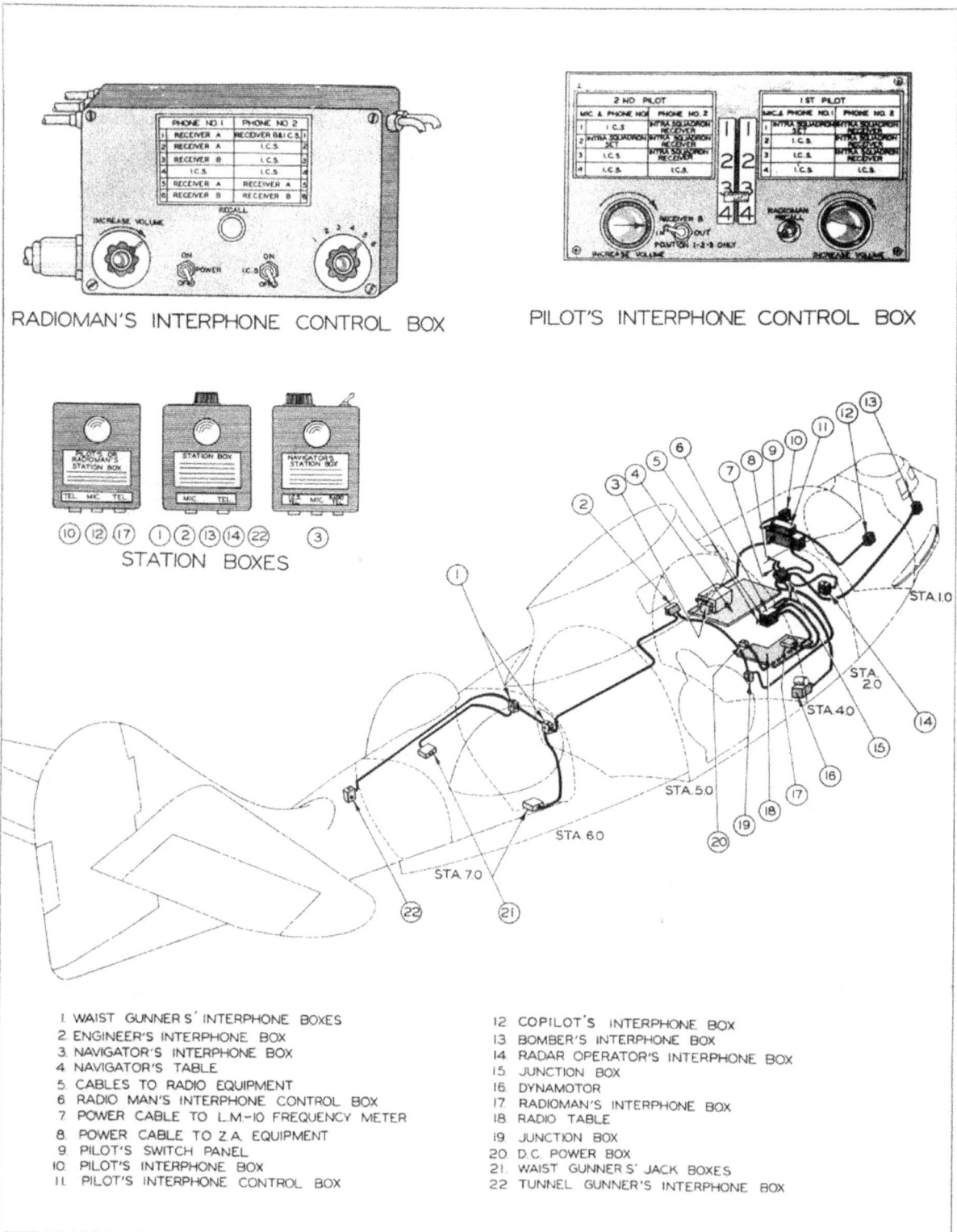

Figure 47—Interphone System Diagram

Section V
Paragraph 3

AN 01-5MA-1

d. OPERATION OF ARB RECEIVER.

WARNING

Certain combinations of the settings of the "HOMING-COMMUN." (band selector) switch and the "M.V.C.-A.V.C." switch cannot be obtained. This is a normal condition and no attempt should be made to force these switches into any position to which they cannot be moved by normal pressure.

(1) TO PLACE RECEIVER IN OPERATION.—Pilot moves the "M.V.C.-A.V.C." (type of reception) switch on pilot's control box to position which indicates the type of reception desired.

(2) TO RECEIVE MCW SIGNALS.—Move the "M.V.C.-A.V.C." switch to "MCW" position. Set the "HOMING-COMMUN." switch to the position corresponding to the frequency range and type of antenna desired. (Settings under "HOMING" provide loop

1. Antenna Reel
*2. ZA Signal Converter
3. ATB Transmitter
4. Interphone Junction Box
5. RU-19 Receiver
6. Antenna Transfer and Clock Panel
7. LM-10 Frequency Meter
8. Interphone Control Box
9. Radio Operator's ARB Receiver
10. Engine Generator Voltage Regulators
11. A-C Distribution Panel
12. Main Distribution Panel
13. Radio Power Box
14. RU-19 Spare Coils
*15. ZA Impedance Adapter
16. Transmitting Key
17. Radio Operator's ARB Control Box
18. RU-19 Switch Box
19. RU-19 Junction Box
20. RU-19 Dynamotor
21. Demolition Switch
22. Interphone Dynamotor
23. Radio Operator's Interphone Station Box
24. Trailing Antenna Tube
25. Radio Table Projector Light

*Deleted by Service Action

Figure 48—Radio Operator's Station

Section V
Paragraph 3

AN 01-5MA-1

antenna pickup; those under "COMMUN." provide extended antenna pickup.)

(3) When the signal being sought is on either of the two high-frequency bands (i.e., between 1.6 and 9.05 megacycles) or when the tuning head is being tuned to a calibrated frequency setting on these bands in order to locate a signal, move the "M.V.C.-A.V.C." switch to the "BROAD" position. When the desired signal has been located, set the "M.V.C.-A.V.C." switch to the "M.C.W." position, and perform the final tuning to the signal with the sensitivity of the receiver reduced to a practical minimum (i.e., keep the volume at the lowest setting that still retains the signal at a comfortable level in the headphones).

Note

After switching from AVC to MVC operation or vice versa, it may be necessary to readjust the volume to regain a satisfactory volume at the headphones.

(4) TO USE AUTOMATIC VOLUME CONTROL.—Tune signal (with pilot's remote tuner) for a maximum output. If automatic volume control is desired, reset the "M.V.C.-A.V.C." switch to the desired position under "A.V.C." and readjust the volume control for the desired output level at the headphones.

(5) TO INCREASE OR REDUCE VOLUME.—Rotate the volume control knob, which is located at the top of the pilot's control box, in a clockwise direction to increase volume (or sensitivity) and in a counterclockwise direction to decrease volume (or sensitivity).

(6) TO RECEIVE CW SIGNALS.—Turn the "M.C.V.-A.V.C." switch on the pilot's control box to the "CW" position. Set the "HOMING-COMMUN." switch to the desired frequency band. Tune in the desired signal at a reduced receiver sensitivity, and then readjust the volume control until the desired signal level is obtained in the headphones. Automatic volume control cannot be obtained during the reception of CW signals.

Note

It is recommended that the extended antenna be connected when the desired signal is being located, since the loop may be so oriented that it will pick up little or none of the signal. When the signal has been located, the "HOMING-COMMUN." switch may be turned to one of the frequency bands under "HOMING."

(7) TO TURN OFF THE RECEIVER.—Turn the "M.V.C.-A.V.C." switch on the pilot's control box to the "OFF" position.

e. OPERATION OF GO-9 TRANSMITTER.

WARNING

Operation of this equipment involves the use of high voltages which are dangerous to life. Operating personnel must at all times observe all safety regulations. Do not change tubes or make adjustments inside equipment with high voltage supply on. Do not depend on door switches or interlocks for protection but always shut down motor-generator or other power equipment. Under certain conditions dangerous potentials may exist in circuits with power controls in the off position due to charges retained by capacitors, etc. To avoid casualties always discharge and ground circuits prior to touching them. Great care should be exercised when operating the equipment with any of the shields removed for purposes of observation or bench testing.

The main power switch should be turned "OFF" and the high voltage circuits grounded before any internal part is touched by the bare hand.

Caution should be observed when operating this equipment for test purposes in the vicinity of other transmitting equipment. Due to the relatively high power output of this equipment, operation in the vicinity of other transmitting equipment may cause flash-over or arcs in the remote equipment should the antenna be resonant. Testing should be done on $\frac{1}{4}$ power under this condition.

(1) COMPARISON OF COMMUNICATION BY C.W. AND M.C.W.

(a) C.W. TELEGRAPHY.

This method provides the greatest distance range, and gives the least interference, both in the immediate vicinity of the transmitter and at a distance. Because of its sharper tuning, it is more difficult, when slightly off frequency, to establish initial communication by C.W. than by M.C.W.

(b) M.C.W. TELEGRAPHY.

This method is most valuable as an auxiliary to C.W. transmission during conditions of fading. Also, during initial calls and at other times when the transmitting operator is uncertain whether the receiver standing by for him is in oscillating (heterodyne) condition, transmission by M.C.W. would appear the preferable method. After establishing communication by M.C.W., if communication is poor, a shift to C.W. generally results in improvement. When the emitted carrier lacks frequency stability due to excessive vibration or other causes, the M.C.W. method may be preferable to C.W.

(2) DISTANCE-FREQUENCY CHART.—The following table is based upon general experience with high frequencies and aircraft communication. Communication conditions on these frequencies may show ap-

AN 01-5MA-1

1. ATB Transmitter
°2. ZA Receiver
°3. ZA Junction Box
4. Interphone Junction Box
°5. ZA Signal Converter
6. Antenna Transfer and Clock Panel
7. LM-10 Frequency Meter
8. RU-19 Junction Box
9. RU-19 Receiver
10. Radio Power Junction Box
11. GO-9 Transmitter

° Deleted by Service Action

Figure 49—Radio Equipment, Showing GO-9 Transmitter

preciable variation from day to day. For any given distance, the best order of frequency not only varies with the time of day, but it is also somewhat lower in the winter time than during the summer. Average frequency ranges for best results over various communication distances are estimated below.

Distance Miles	Estimated Best Frequency Kcs.		
	Mid-day	Dawn or Dusk	Night
0-50	3,000-4,525	3,000-4,525	3,000-4,525
50-150	3,000-4,000	3,000-4,000	3,000-4,000
150-250	4,000-6,000	3,500-4,525	3,000-4,000
250-400	6,000-8,000	4,000-6,000	3,500-4,525
400-600	6,000-9,050	4,500-7,000	4,000-6,000
600-1,000	8,000-9,050	6,000-8,000	4,500-7,000

(3) PRELIMINARY ADJUSTMENT — GENERAL.—Before applying any power or attempting any preliminary adjustment of the equipment, the "POWER" switch on the Rectifier Unit should be checked to see that it is in the "OFF" position. The "A-C VOLTAGE COMPENSATION" switches should all be "ON." The "POWER CONTROL" switch should be in the "TUNE" position. The "TRANSMITTER SELECTOR" switch should be set either to "H.F." or "I. F.", depending on which transmitter is to be operated. As the adjustment of the High Frequency Transmitter will be discussed first, this switch should be placed in the "H.F." position. The "EMISSION" switch should be set for "C.W." operation.

(4) PRELIMINARY ADJUSTMENT OF HIGH FREQUENCY TRANSMITTER.—The radio frequency adjustments must generally be made after the power is applied. However, the master oscillator range switch, "M.O. RANGE" Control "A"; master oscillator tuning control, "M.O. TUNING" Control "B"; doubler circuit range switch "DOUBLER RANGE" Control "C"; doubler circuit tuning control, "DOUBLER TUNING" Control "D"; intermediate amplifier range switch, "I.A. RANGE" Control "E"; and intermediate amplifier circuit tuning control, "INT. AMP. TUNING" Control "F" may be set by reference to the calibration chart. The power amplifier circuit tuning control, "P.A. TUNING" Control "G," may also be set approximately to frequency by the calibrated dial. The "ANT. COUPLING" Control "K," should be set to zero. After checking the controls as above (assuming that the power supply is in operation), the "POWER" switch on the Rectifier Unit should be moved to the "ON" position. This should cause the "FILAMENT VOLTS" meter on the "Rectifier Unit" to indicate. The voltmeter should be adjusted to indicate 10 volts, or to the red line, by turning the control marked "FILAMENT" until the meter indicates properly.

The flame-proof telegraph key with cable and plug should be inserted in the keying circuit by means of the KEY jack. Pressing the key should energize the keying relay. This applies 500 volts from the auxiliary rectifier to the master oscillator and intermediate amplifier circuits. If the keying relay does not operate, the side shields of both transmitters and the tube access door on the Rectifier Unit should be inspected to see that the interlock circuits are properly closed.

Press the telegraph key and resonate the doubler tuning circuit by means of the "DOUBLER TUNING" Control "D." Resonance will be indicated by maximum grid current on the intermediate amplifier grid current meter ("I.A. GRID CURRENT"). Next, resonate the intermediate amplifier circuit by means of the "INT. AMP. TUNING" Control "F." Resonance will be indicated by maximum grid current on the power amplifier grid current meter ("P.A. GRID CURRENT"). Set the "POWER CONTROL" switch on the Rectifier Unit to the ¼ tap. When the key is pressed this will apply approximately 1,200 volts to the plate of the power amplifier tube. Press the key and resonate the power amplifier circuit. This is best accomplished by first setting the reading on "P.A. TUNING" Control "G" as closely as possible to the frequency desired by the calibrated dial and then, while observing the power amplifier plate current meter, "P.A. PLATE CURRENT" located in the Rectifier Unit, turn the control knob "G" in the direction which decreases the plate current. Adjust control "G" until the plate current dips downward to a minimum value. When the doubler circuit, intermediate amplifier and power amplifier circuits have been properly resonated the intermediate amplifier grid current meter, "I.A. GRID CURRENT," will indicate approximately 6 milliamperes, while the power amplifier grid current meter, "P.A. GRID CURRENT," will indicate approximately 40 milliamperes, and the power amplifier plate current meter, "P.A. PLATE CURRENT," will indicate approximately 45 milliamperes.

If the antenna that is connected to the transmitter is known to be an approximate half-wave for the frequency used, the "ANTENNA FEED" Control "H," should be set in the "VOLTAGE" or No. 2 position. If the antenna is approximately ¼ or ¾ of a wave-length long, the "ANTENNA FEED" Control "H," should be set in the "CURRENT" of No. 1 position.

Assuming that the antenna is a half-wave, the following is the procedure for tuning the antenna circuit. Adjust the antenna coupling, "ANT. COUPLING" Control "K," to approximately 25 divisions. Set the antenna tuning capacitor, "ANT. TUNING CAPACITOR" Control "I," at approximately 25 divisions. Set the antenna feed switch, "ANTENNA FEED" Control "H," in the "VOLTAGE" or No. 2 position. Press the key and rotate the knob of the antenna tuning inductance, "ANT. INDUCTANCE" Control "J," until a rise in power amplifier plate current, "P.A. PLATE CURRENT," is noted. If no point can be found in the tuning of Control "J" that gives a rise in the "P.A. PLATE CURRENT" meter, set the antenna tuning "CAPACITOR" Control "I," to another value of capacity and repeat the tuning process with the antenna tuning inductance, "ANT. INDUCTANCE" Control

"J." When the point has been found at which resonance occurs and both Controls "I" and "J" have been adjusted for maximum indication on the power amplifier plate current meter, readjust the antenna coupling, "ANT. COUPLING" Control "K," until the power amplifier plate current meter indicates approximately 100 milliamperes. The power amplifier tuning, "P.A. TUNING" Control "G," should be readjusted for minimum power amplifier plate current each time the antenna tuning controls are changed.

(5) FINAL ADJUSTMENT OF HIGH FREQUENCY TRANSMITTER.—With the equipment operating satisfactorily on the ¼ power tap, set the "POWER CONTROL" switch to "FULL" power. Pressing the key will apply 2,000 volts to the plate of the power amplifier tube. Press the key and readjust the power amplifier tuning, "P.A. TUNING" Control "G," antenna tuning, "ANT. TUNING CAPACITOR" Control "I," "ANT. INDUCTANCE" Control "J," and antenna coupling, "ANT. COUPLING" Control "K" for optimum adjustment. The power amplifier plate current meter "P.A. PLATE CURRENT" should not exceed the red line or 175 milliamperes. The voltage compensation switches, "A.C. VOLTAGE COMPENSATION," on the Rectifier Unit should now be set so that keying the transmitter does not cause the voltage, as indicated by the filament voltmeter, "FILAMENT VOLTS," to fluctuate more than approximately 0.2 volt. These voltage compensation switches connect different amounts of capacity in series with the 800 cycle supply line. The correct amount of capacity will compensate for the varying power factor which is caused by the change in load on the generator when the transmitter key is closed, and will therefore improve the regulation of the power equipment. In general, it has been found that a capacitance of approximately 4 microfarads is the correct compensation for full load operation. This is in addition to the 8 microfarads of fixed capacity that are continuously connected in the circuit.

When all adjustments are considered satisfactory they may be recorded for future reference. It is desirable also that the operator note all meter readings and other observations which may aid in resetting the equipment.

For tuning the equipment with a ¼ or ¾ wave antenna, the procedure is the same as for tuning with a ½ wave antenna except that the voltage-current feed switch, "ANTENNA FEED" Control "H," is set in the "CURRENT" or No. 1 position. Tuning the antenna should be accomplished by tuning for maximum power amplifier plate current, not to exceed 175 ma. on full power, with the antenna tuning controls, and for minimum power amplifier plate current with the power amplifier tuning control. When the equipment is correctly tuned in the "VOLTAGE FEED" position there will only be a small indication of antenna current on the R.F. ammeter. When the antenna is tuned in the "CURRENT FEED" position the procedure is the same but there will be an appreciable amount of antenna current on the R.F. ammeter. In either case the power is being delivered to the antenna.

CAUTION

Do not operate the power amplifier plate current at a value greater than 175 milliamperes as indicated by the red line on the meter. ("P.A. PLATE CURRENT").

(6) PRELIMINARY ADJUSTMENT OF INTERMEDIATE FREQUENCY TRANSMITTER.—Set the TRANSMITTER SELECTOR switch on the rectifier unit to the "I.F." position. Set the "POWER CONTROL" switch to the "TUNE" position. The master oscillator range switch, "M.O. RANGE" Control "A," the master oscillator tuning, "M.O. TUNING" Control "B," the power amplifier range switch, "P.A. RANGE" Control "C" may be set to the desired frequency by reference to the calibration chart. Set the antenna coupling, "ANT. COUPLING" Control "H," to the minimum or zero position. With the power supply in operation, closing the power switch on the rectifier unit and pressing the transmitter key will apply power to the transmitter unit. With the "POWER CONTROL" switch in the "TUNE" position, approximately 500 volts will be applied to the plate circuit of the master oscillator and intermediate amplifier. The power amplifier grid current meter, "P.A. GRID CURRENT," should indicate approximately 40 milliamperes. Set the "POWER CONTROL" switch on the Rectifier Unit to the ¼ power position. Press the telegraph key and resonate the power amplifier circuit by means of P.A. "TUNING" Control "D" for minimum power amplifier plate current as indicated on the "P.A. PLATE CURRENT" meter in the rectifier unit. Under this condition, pressing of the key applies approximately 1,200 volts to the plate of the power amplifier tube. In the resonance position, the power amplifier plate current meter should be indicating approximately 45 milliamperes. To adjust the antenna circuit, first set the antenna coupling, "ANT. COUPLING" Control "H," to approximately 30 divisions. Set the "ANT. LOAD" Control "E" on Step No. 1 and set the "ANTENNA TUNING STEP" Control "F," on tap No. 1 and rotate the antenna tuning control "ANT. TUNING" Control "G" throughout the range of the dial from 0 to 100 divisions. If no indications of a rise in power amplifier plate current is noted on the "P.A. PLATE CURRENT" meter, set the "ANTENNA TUNING STEP" Control "F," on tap No. 2 and repeat the rotation of the "ANT. TUNING" Control "G." Repeat the process on each step of Control "F" until a rise in the power amplifier plate current is noted. If no condition is found that will give the desired rise in power amplifier plate current, set the "ANT. LOAD" Control "E," on Step No. 2 and repeat the tuning process with Controls "F" and "G." If a rise in plate current still does not occur, repeat with Control "E" on Step No. 3. When the res-

onance point has been found, adjust the antenna coupling, "ANT. COUPLING" Control "H," until the power amplifier plate current is 100 milliamperes.

(7) FINAL ADJUSTMENT OF INTERMEDIATE FREQUENCY TRANSMITTER.—With the equipment operating satisfactorily on the ¼ power tap, set the "POWER CONTROL" Switch to the "FULL" power position and press the key. This will apply 2,000 volts to the plate of the power amplifier tube. Adjust the antenna coupling, "ANT. COUPLING" Control "H," until the power amplifier plate current is 175 milliamperes as indicated on "P.A. PLATE CURRENT" meter (pointer at the red line). Check the adjustment of the power amplifier tuning for best over-all condition.

When these adjustments are considered satisfactory, they may be recorded for future reference. It is desirable, also, that the operator note all meter readings and other observations which may aid in resetting the equipment.

(8) OPERATION WITH FIXED ANTENNA.—When operating the intermediate frequency transmitter into a fixed antenna, it will be necessary to connect in the extra load coil, provided in the transmitter, if the frequency to be used is below 400 kilocycles. This is accomplished by connecting the jumper, which is supplied, between the trailing wire antenna post and the input to the fixed antenna loading inductance. The fixed antenna is connected to the fixed antenna output post. The antenna tuning adjustments, as previously described, also apply when operating with the fixed antenna. When receiving at some frequencies, the loading inductance in series with the antenna will resonate with other circuit components and will act as a wave trap to block out signals on these frequencies. For this reason, when using the antenna for reception in conjunction with the intermediate frequency transmitter, the antenna load switch should be set on tap No. 4 (minimum loading) and the extra antenna load coil should be removed from the circuit.

CAUTION

When using the fixed antenna for intermediate frequency transmitter operation, extreme caution should be taken to keep the fixed antenna lead-out well in the clear of other objects, as the voltages built up on the fixed antenna are extremely high. In general, the trailing wire antenna should be used for intermediate frequency operation, whenever possible.

(9) FREQUENCY ADJUSTMENT FACILITIES.—A binding post is provided on the high frequency and intermediate frequency transmitter, marked "C.F.I.," for connection to a crystal frequency indicator. This binding post is connected to the master oscillator through a ground circuit in such a manner that sufficient energy will be provided to the crystal frequency indicator to allow easy adjustment of the master oscillator to the desired frequency. It will be noted that on the high frequency transmitter CAY-52193, Control "A" has two sets of calibrations; the right-hand set is the output frequencies of the transmitter and the left-hand set, the operating frequency of the oscillator. The latter calibrations are for use only with the "C.F.I." During checking or calibration of frequency, the "POWER CONTROL" switch on the rectifier unit should be in the "TUNE" position. If desired, the receiver can also be used to monitor the transmitter to the same frequency as some received signal. This is accomplished by first tuning the receiver on "C.W.," then "zero" beat with the incoming signal. Then, after first withdrawing the side tone plug from the receiver switch box and plugging the former directly into the latter, the (Manual) volume control setting of the receiver is reduced and the transmitter master oscillator frequency varied until it is set to "zero" beat with the receiver, then its frequency equals that of the previously received signal. In order to avoid false settings, due to beat notes from harmonics, it is necessary that the operator assure himself, by the approximate calibration of the transmitter, that he is near the desired frequency before obtaining the exact setting with the aid of the crystal frequency indicator or the receiver. After tuning the master oscillator to the correct frequency, the "POWER CONTROL" switch should be turned to the ¼ power position and the intermediate amplifier and power amplifier tuning control should be adjusted for optimum operation.

(10) MODULATED CONTINUOUS WAVE OPERATION.—After the transmitters have been adjusted as previously described for "C.W." operation, they may be operated on "M.C.W." by setting the "EMISSION" switch to "M.C.W." No other change in adjustment is required.

(11) SIDE TONE VOLUME CONTROL.—With the transmitter in operation the amount of side tone delivered to the receiver can be varied by the "SIDE TONE" volume control on the rectifier unit. Turning the control clockwise increases the output of the side tone which should be adjusted for noise levels encountered in flight.

(12) LENGTH OF ANTENNA.—The specification of the antenna for which this equipment was designed are: fixed "V" antennae; fore and aft antennae; trailing wire antennae not exceeding 350 feet long. The "V" antenna consists of a wire from the left wing to the vertical fin to the right wing. The distance across the open end of the "V" along the wing is approximately 104 feet. The lead-in may be from either leg of the "V," direct as possible to the transmitter unit.

The trailing wire antenna is the most satisfactory antenna for both units if maximum power output and strong signals are desired. In general, the longer the antenna, the greater will be the output power.

When using the intermediate frequency transmitter, the trailing wire antenna may be made any convenient length. However, an antenna as long as practical should be used since the shorter antennae develop high voltages which may become dangerous.

When using the trailing wire antenna with the high frequency transmitter, increased radiation will be secured if the antenna is one quarter, three quarter or five quarter wave lengths long for the frequency being used.

A table of recommended antenna lengths is given below. The use of shorter antennae is possible but is not recommended as a short antenna is very inefficient and builds up tremendous voltages within the transmitter. Such high voltages may arc to the frame or shields of the equipment causing damage or burning out fuses. These dangerous voltages will also be present on the antenna lead-in when using short antennae and if arc-over occurs, there is danger of fire. When occasion demands the use of a very short antenna, operate on LOW POWER if possible for safety's sake.

TABLE OF RECOMMENDED ANTENNA LENGTHS FOR TRAILING WIRE ANTENNA

Frequency	Length
3,000 kcs.	210 feet
4,000 kcs.	150 feet
5,000 kcs.	120 feet
6,000 kcs.	100 feet
7,000 kcs.	85 feet
8,000 kcs.	70 feet
10,000 kcs.	55 feet
12,000 kcs.	45 feet
14,000 kcs.	35 feet

The above antenna lengths, which are slightly below three quarter wave resonance, have been chosen, since in general they give more satisfactory communication range than one quarter wave resonant antenna.

(13) ROUTINE OPERATION. — When the high frequency and intermediate frequency transmitters have been tuned to the frequencies desired, the normal routine operation of this equipment is as follows:

(a) Move the "TRANSMITTER SELECTOR" switch on rectifier unit to the transmitter unit desired.

(b) Place the "POWER" switch in the "ON" position and check the filament voltmeter to see that it is indicating normal voltage.

(c) No other adjustments are normally required, but it is desirable that the antenna current and plate current meters be occasionally observed to see if their indications are normal.

During normal operation, and for short standby periods the "POWER" switch may be left in the "ON" position. However, at the completion of a communication, or if there is to be a long period of inactivity of the equipment, the "POWER" switch should be moved to the "OFF" position.

(14) CHANGING FREQUENCIES.—The following is the procedure required for shifting from one frequency to another:

(a) High Frequency Transmitter Type CAY 52193.

1. Unlock all tuning dials.
2. Set "M.O. RANGE" Control "A."
3. Set "M.O. TUNING" Control "B."
4. Set "DOUBLER RANGE" Control "C."
5. Set "DOUBLER TUNING" Control "D."
6. Set "I.A. RANGE" Control "E."
7. Set "INT. ANT. TUNING" Control "F."
8. Set "P.A. TUNING" Control "G."
9. Set "ANTENNA FEED" Control "H."
10. Set "ANT. TUNING CAPACITOR" Control "I."
11. Set "ANT. INDUCTANCE" Control "J."
12. Set "ANT. COUPLING" Control "K."

(b) Intermediate Frequency Transmitter Type CAY 52192.

1. Unlock all tuning dials.
2. Set "M.O. RANGE" Control "A."
3. Set "M.O. TUNING" Control "B."
4. Set "P.A. RANGE" Control "C."
5. Set "P.A. TUNING" Control "D."
6. Set "ANT. LOAD" Control "E."
7. Set "ANTENNA TUNING STEP" Control "F."
8. Set "ANT. TUNING" Control "G."
9. Set "ANT. COUPLING" Control "H."
10. If the fixed antenna is used, connect the jumper between the trailing wire output post and the fixed antenna input post and connect the fixed antenna to the fixed antenna output post.

(15) POWER OUTPUT RATING.—The power output rating of the Navy Model GO-9 Aircraft Radio Transmitting Equipment is as follows:

	Frequency	Watts C.W.	Watts M.C.W.
Below 15,000 feet			
Trailing Wire Antenna	300-600	100	70
	3,000-13,000	125	87.5
	13,000-18,000	100	70
Fixed Antenna	300-600	50	35
	3,000-18,000	50	35
Above 15,000 feet			
Trailing Wire Antenna	300-600	70	49
	3,000-18,000	100	70
Fixed Antenna	300-450	10	7
	450-600	20	14
	3,000-18,000	40	28

The actual power output of the equipment will vary greatly depending on the efficiency of antennae used and will generally be much greater than the rated power output.

(16) RESET ACCURACY.—The reset accuracy of the equipment is such that after adjusting the transmitter for operation at any frequency within its range,

noting settings, and then completely detuning, it will be possible to reset the transmitter when an accuracy of 0.02% when approaching the setting in either direction. For best accuracy, however, it is good policy to make final adjustments in the direction in which the dial reading increases.

f. OPERATION OF RU-19 RECEIVER.

(1) Plug a coil set into the receiver which will cover the frequency range desired. Ranges of coil sets are as follows:

Single Coil Set, Range "D" 850-1330 kc

Single Coil Set, Range "E" 1330-2040 kc

Single Coil Set, Range "F" 2040-3000 kc

Single Coil Set, Range "H" 4000-6000 kc

Single Coil Set, Range "K" 9050-13575 kc

Dual Coil Set, Range "O" 195-290 kc and Range "P" 290-435 kc

Dual Coil Set, Range "Q" 540-830 kc and Range "G" 3000-4525 kc

Dual Coil Set, Range "Q" 540-830 kc and Range "M" 5200-7700 kc

Dual Coil Set, Range "L" 400-600 kc and Range "N" 6000-9050 kc

Dual Coil Set, Range "Q" 540-830 kc and Range "F" 2040-3000 kc

(2) Switch on power at either switch box by turning volume control selector switch to either "AUTO" or "MANUAL," according to whether automatic or manual volume control is desired. Dynamotor will start.

(3) Plug head set into switch box.

(4) Set toggle switch to "MCW" or "CW" as desired.

Note

For comparison of CW and MCW signals, see operation of GO-9 transmitter, Paragraph *e*, (1), preceding.

The automatic gain control tube holds the level of the audio output in the telephone receivers at a substantially constant level for all values of incoming radio signal strength above a certain minimum. Thus when the control selector switch is in "AUTO" position, this constant audio output may be varied by use of the volume-control knob, but it cannot be increased above the level to which it is set.

A weak audio output in the telephone receivers, when receiving strong radio signal in the "AUTO" position may indicate insufficient modulation in the transmitted wave. But in making tests by comparing the audio output of the receiver on "AUTO" with the output on "MANUAL" it should be borne in mind that for strong incoming radio signals the 50 milliwatts of audio output which represents the "AUTO" control level may sound considerably weaker than the output which is heard on "MANUAL." For example, if the incoming radio wave is of sufficient magnitude to give the maximum output on "MANUAL," which is 300-500 milliwatts, the power output in the telephones may drop by a factor of 10 to one when the switch is thrown to "AUTO." This in itself is an indication that the receiver automatic gain control is operating normally.

If the distance from the transmitting station is steadily increased, the output level on "MANUAL" will gradually decrease (remaining constant on "AUTO") until it reaches the level of 50-60 milliwatts which characterizes the output on "AUTO." If the incoming radio wave becomes still weaker, from this point on, the audio output on "AUTO" will decrease, together with the output on "MANUAL."

A test meter is supplied with the receiver. The test meter is a d-c milliammeter, scale 0-35 milliamperes, in a suitable carrying case. The cable is a two-wire cord with a plug on the end which may be plugged into the switch box at the jack marked "METER."

When the D-W loop is used for reception, the test meter can be used as a bearing indicator. The meter gives a visual indication of the bearing of the transmitting station by reading a maximum of current when the loop is set in its position of minimum received signal.

For satisfactory direction finding or homing operations on the loop the signal should be received in the "CW" position regardless of whether the transmission is modulated or not. If using the test meter as a bearing indicator, set volume control selector switch to "AUTO."

g. AN/APN-1 RADIO ALTIMETER.

(See figures 3, 4 and 50.)

(1) GENERAL.—The model AN/APN-1 Radio Altimeter equipment is designed to provide direct indication of altitude relative to the terrain during flight. The equipment is provided with a double range indicator to allow altimeter readings from zero to 400 ft or 400 to 4,000 feet.

CAUTION

1. Operating personnel are not to disturb any of the screwdriver adjustments on the front panel of the Radio Transmitter-Receiver. These adjustments are accessible externally only for the convenience of qualified installation or maintenance personnel when calibrating the equipment.

2. The high range of the altimeter must not be used when flying at altitudes within the low range, or when landing. The high range is not calibrated for such use and an accurate zero altitude indication would not be obtained.

3. When the aircraft is resting on the ground, the Altitude Indicator pointer may not indicate zero altitude. Never attempt to adjust the equipment to obtain a zero reading for this condition.

(2) OPERATIONAL CHECK.

(a) Place "RADIO" switch on the pilot's switch panel to the "ON" position.

(b) Rotate power switch knob on the Indicator in the "ON" direction. After allowing approximately one minute for the tubes to heat, observe that the pointer of the Altitude Indicator has moved from its sub-zero stop position, indicating that the equipment is energized.

(c) Place the "RANGE" switch on the Altitude Indicator to the high range or low range, depending upon the altitude of the airplane. (See second paragraph at Caution note following *g*, (1) above.)

(d) Rotate the Altitude Limit Switch to the desired altitude setting. This setting determines the altitude at which the Radio-Transmitter-Receiver will actuate the Altitude Limit Indicator lights.

(e) Altitude Indicator will give true indications of altitude, over the entire range of the equipment, when flying over rough or uneven terrain, or when flying through bumpy air.

ment is protected against damage from short-circuits by a fuse of three-ampere rating located at the lower right-hand corner of the front panel of the Radio Transmitter-Receiver. A spare fuse of corresponding rating is provided in an adjacent receptacle.

IMPORTANT

If necessary to make any substitution for the fuses (type 4AC Littlefuse) which are supplied with the equipment and spare parts, use "slow-blowing" fuses of the same current capacity if available. If not available, substitute fuses of the next higher current rating for TEMPORARY EMERGENCY USE ONLY.

h. RADAR EQUIPMENT.—Operation of the following Navy aircraft radar equipment can be found in CONFIDENTIAL operating instructions manuals:

AN/APX-2—AN 08-10-192

AN/APS-3—AN 08-10-196

4. ARMAMENT.

a. BOW GUNS.—On BuAer Serial Number 46580, two .30 calibre machine guns are mounted on a plexiglas shell in a revolving circular windshield. Earlier airplanes mounted a single .30 calibre machine gun

Figure 50—Radio Altimeter Transceiver

(3) ALTITUDE LIMIT INDICATOR.—This auxiliary device relieves the pilot of the constant attention to the Altitude Indicator scale. It consists of three colored lamps, one of which is illuminated for each of the three conditions of relay contact operation.

(a) RED.—Indicates flight below the preset altitude control range determined by the Altitude Limit Switch setting.

(b) WHITE.—Indicates flight within the preset altitude control range.

(c) GREEN.—Indicates flight above the preset altitude control range.

(4) FUSES.—The AN/APN-1 Altimeter equip-

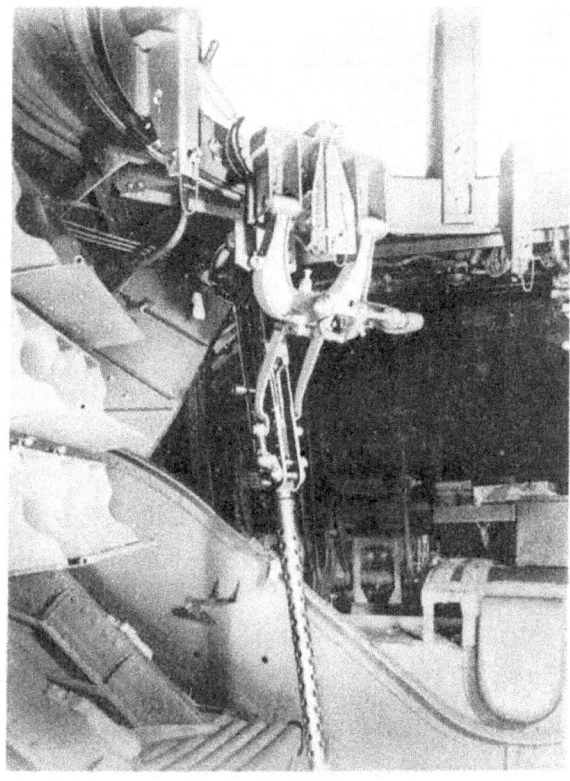

Figure 51—Bow Gun—Stowed

which fires through a similar revolving windshield.

(1) SINGLE GUN TURRET.
(a) STOWING.
(See figure 51.)

1. Elevate the gun to a vertical position.

2. Rotate the windshield to the right until it hits the stop.

3. Unlock the stirrup, retract the gun, and swing it inboard.

4. Place the muzzle in the socket aft of the firing step and lock the spade grip to the bracket on bulkhead 1.

5. Lock the turret with the friction lock (left of gun mount).

6. Slide the slot cover in place.

7. Snap the manhole cover harness snaps into the eyebolts on the windshield on the straight side of the manhole.

8. Swing the cover up and lock with toggle locks along the rim.

(b) TO READY FOR FIRING.—Reverse the procedure outlined above. (See figure 52.)

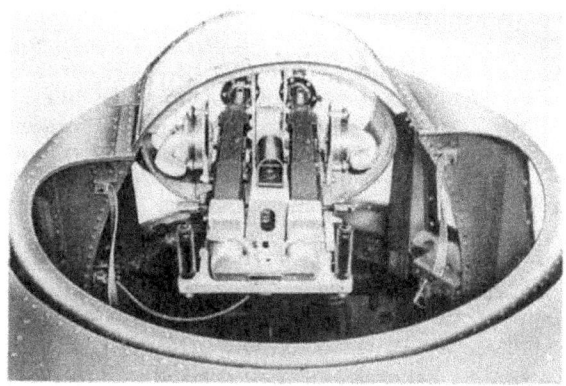

Figure 53—Bow Guns in Firing Position

3. Depress the guns until they hit the stop.

4. Pass the strap that is fastened to the enclosure bulkhead underneath the adapter and pull up tight.

(b) TO READY FOR FIRING.—The bow guns are readied for firing by unfastening the stowage strap. (See figure 53.)

b. SIDE WAIST GUNS.
(See figures 54 and 55.)

(1) FIRING GUARD.—A firing guard is provided for each side gun, to prevent the gun from being fired into the tail or the after portion of the hull. The firing guard consists of a ¾ inch steel tube attached to the hull just below the tear drop gun blister. When the rotating shield of the gun blister is raised for firing the gun, the firing guard is lifted and attached to the clamp on the rotating shield. Before the gun blister is closed, the firing guard must be placed in its stowed position. (See figure 55.)

Figure 52—Bow Gun in Firing Position

(2) TWIN GUN TURRET.—To the right of the gunner, provisions are made to stow four ammunition containers of 350 rounds capacity. Two more ammunition containers are installed on the mount, making a total of 2100 rounds of ammunition.

(a) STOWING.

1. Rotate the windshield until the guns are pointed directly forward.

2. Lock the enclosure with the function lock located to the left of the gun mount.

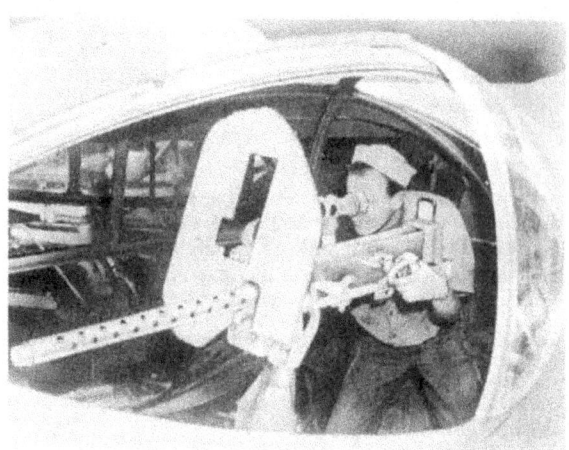

Figure 54—Waist Gun in Firing Position

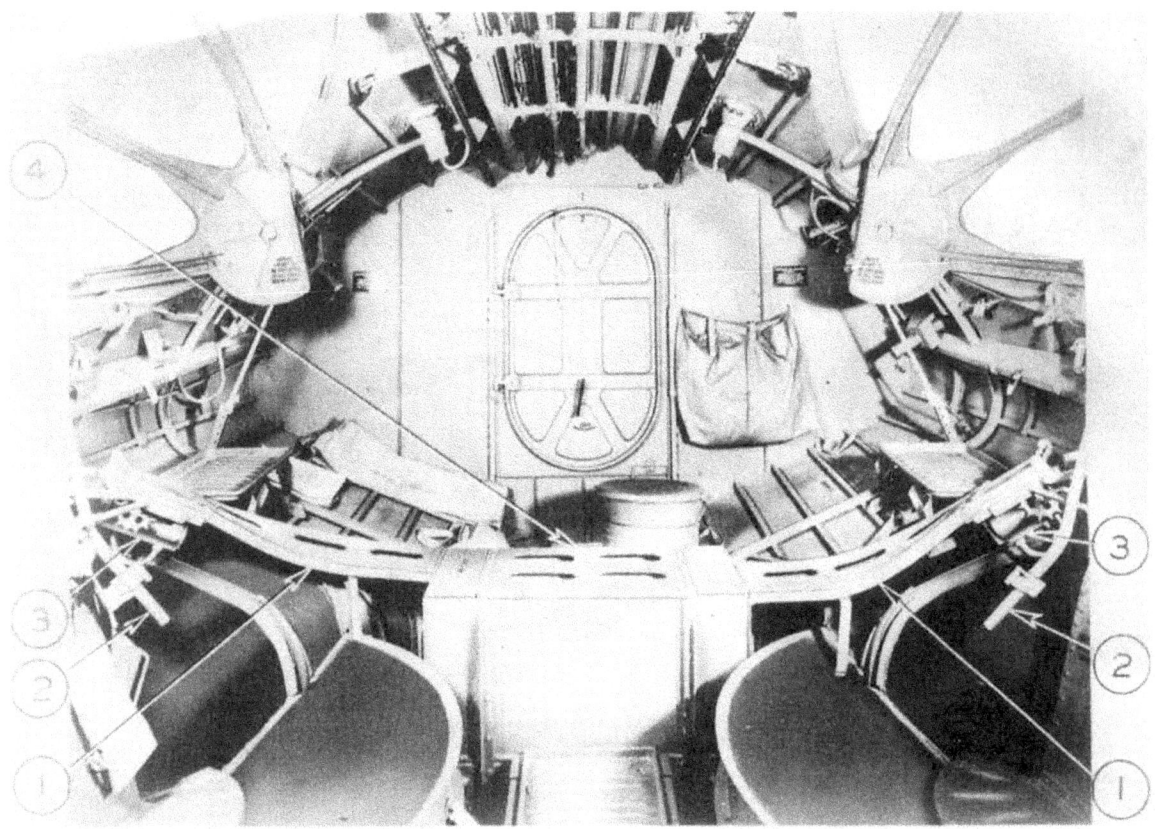

1. Ammunition Feed Chutes
2. Firing Guards
3. Assist Motors
4. Ammunition Magazine

Figure 55—Side Gun Feed Mechanism

(2) STOWED POSITION.—The gun is stowed on the mount in a fore-and-aft position. The muzzle rests in a cradle and is secured with a metal strip. To stow the gun:

Swing the gun inside the airplane with the muzzle pointing aft.

Close and lock rotating shield of transparent gun blister.

Secure the muzzle stabilizer with the metal strap.

With the strap provided, secure the rear portion of the gun to the anchor located aft of bulkhead 6.

When closed, the transparent gun blisters are kept watertight by inflatable sealing tubes. A valve for releasing the air in the sealing tubes is integral with each latch. A hand pump for inflating the sealing tubes is stowed aft of the port blister. Instructions for operating the waterseals are on both sides of the aft bulkhead. *(See figure 22.)*

Switches controlling the continuous feed ammunition boosters *(See figure 55)* are on either side of the hull, forward of the gun mounts. Power switches for the gun camera receptacles are near the gun booster switches. Before either the gun booster or the gun cameras will operate, the line switches on the main distribution panel must be set for the proper bus.

c. TUNNEL GUN.

(1) To place the gun in firing position: *(See figure 57.)*

Unlatch the tunnel door, swing it up into vertical position, and fasten door with the catch.

Unlatch the spade grip.

Swing the gun and stirrup up out of the stowed position.

Section V

AN 01-5MA-1

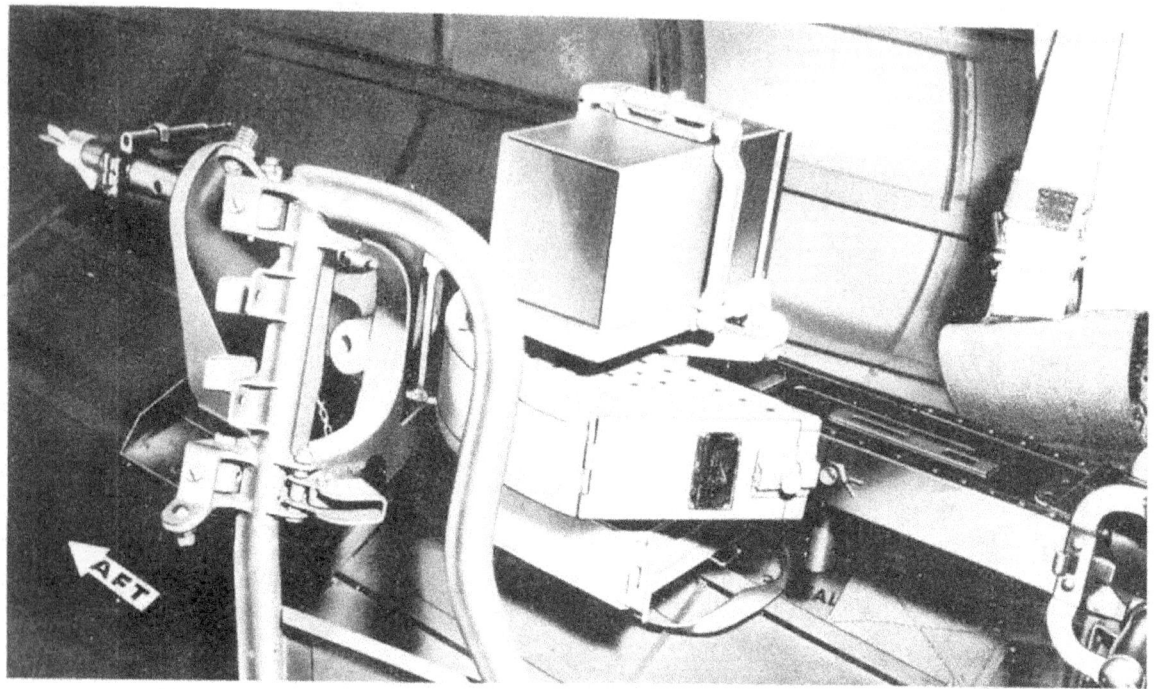

Figure 56—Tunnel Gun—Stowed

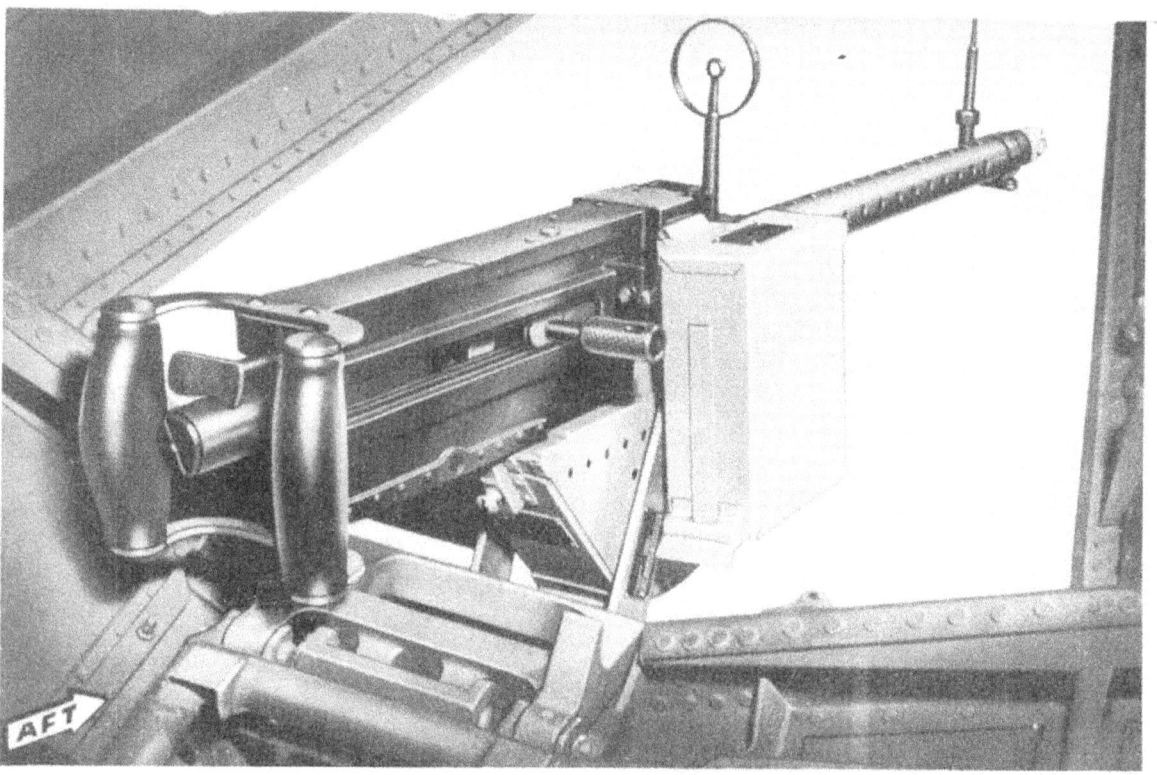

Figure 57—Tunnel Gun—Ready

Unfasten the toggle lock holding stirrup to Vee brace.

Lower stirrup from vertical position.

Screw the locking nut tight.

(2) To place the gun in stowed position: *(See figure 56.)*

Unscrew the locking nut.

Swing the stirrup into vertical position.

Fasten the stirrup to Vee brace with the toggle lock.

Swing the gun and stirrup above the Vee brace hinge into stowed position at left-hand side of hull.

Place barrel in stowage hook and latch spade grip in place.

Unfasten tunnel door, swing it down into horizontal position, and latch the door.

A gun camera receptacle and switch is on the port side of the hull, adjacent to the hatch. Line switches on the main distribution panel must be on before power will feed through the receptacle.

d. GUN CAMERAS.—Provision is made at each gun position for the installation of a G.S.A.P. camera N-4 B.O. 294389. One camera mount Mk. 3 B.O. 300519 is used at bow gun position and one at tunnel gun position. Two camera mounts Mk. 5 B.O. 300525 are used for the two side waist gun cameras. A special bore sight is furnished as part of the camera equipment, and is used for sighting a lighted target when the camera is being aligned with the gun and sight. To allow for adjustment when boresighting, the camera mount has oversize holes which permit sufficient movement of the camera to bring the line of sight of the camera parallel with the axis of the bore of the gun. After the camera is properly aligned, it is secured by tightening and safetying the bolts.

Camera power receptacles and switches are placed convenient to each gun station. Power will not feed to camera receptacles unless master camera switch on main distribution panel is set for proper bus.

e. BOMB EQUIPMENT.

(1) BOMB LOADS.—The bomb load consists of any one of the following:

Two 1000 pound demolition bombs.

Four 1000 pound demolition bombs.

Four 500 pound demolition bombs.

Eight 325 pound depth bombs, AN Mk 17-2.

Twelve 100 pound demolition bombs.

Two 1935 pound torpedoes, Mk 13 or Mk 13-1, with air stabilizers.

Any of the following 1000 pound class bombs and fuses can be carried in the racks:

Mk 5 with nose fuse Mk 21 and tail fuse Mk 23.

Mk 9 with nose fuse Mk 21 and tail fuse Mk 23.

Mk 13 with nose fuse Mk 21 and tail fuse Mk 23.

Mk 7 water-filled practice bomb.

Figure 58—Torpedo Rack on Port Wing

Any of the following 500 pound class bombs and fuses can be carried in the racks:

Mk 3-1 with nose fuse Mk 21 and tail fuse Mk 23.

Mk 9 with nose fuse Mk 21 and tail fuse Mk 23.

Mk 12 with nose fuse Mk 21 and tail fuse Mk 23.

Mk 5 water-filled practice bomb.

Mk 11 water-filled practice bomb.

Any of the following 100 pound class bombs and fuses can be carried in the racks:

Mk 1-3 with nose fuse Mk 19-1 (This type can be carried in Mk 42 bomb racks only).

Mk 4 with nose fuse Mk 19-1.

Mk 7 water-filled practice bomb.

Mk 15 water-filled practice bomb.

(2) BOMB RACKS.—The service bomb rack installation consists of four bomb racks Mk 51-7. The racks are mounted inside the center section of the wing near the lower skin surface. They are placed, two on each side of the airplane, outboard of the nacelles. Access to the racks is through openings in the bottom of the wing. These racks remain installed in the airplane at all times, even though external racks are installed for carrying torpedoes, depth bombs or 100 pound bombs. On the bomber's switch panel, these four racks are referred to as "Mk 51 INTERNAL."

To carry torpedoes or depth bombs, "Mk 13 Torpedo and External Bomb Racks" (CVAC Dwg. 28A5150) are installed, one left-hand and one right-hand. These racks are mounted outside and below the center section of the wing, one on each side of the airplane, outboard of the wing struts, and inboard of the internal racks. These racks are installed only for a particular mission.

(a) TORPEDO RACK.—The torpedo rack installation includes a "Rack Assembly—External Bombs" (CVAC Dwg. 28A5132—OL and OR). One assembly is installed on left-hand side and one on right-hand side of the airplane. Each assembly consists essentially of members for attaching two bomb racks Mk 51-7 to the wing, together with the necessary electrical and manual control connections, splash fairings, torpedo rack bumper blocks (CVAC Dwg. 28A3037), starting lanyard attaching angle (CVAC Dwg. 28F5340), and torpedo stop bolt installation (CVAC Dwg. 28F3045-50). Each assembly carries one 1935 pound torpedo, Mk 13 or Mk 13-1, with air stabilizer.

(b) EXTERNAL BOMB RACK.—The external bomb rack is basically the same as the torpedo rack, with certain modifications. The torpedo rack bumper blocks, the torpedo stop bolt installation, and the starting lanyard angle are not required.

In addition to the Mk 51-7 rack, provision is made for the installation of four Mk 42 practice racks. These racks are installed only for a particular mission, and are not normally installed on the airplane. They are suspended externally beneath the wing, two in tandem on each side of the center line. Three 100 pound bombs per rack, or twelve in all, are carried on the Mk 42 racks.

The installation positions of the external racks, both Mk 42 and Mk 51-7, are marked on the under side of the wing.

(3) BOMBER'S COMPARTMENT.—The bomber's compartment is located forward of the pilot's compartment in the nose of the airplane.

Provision is made for the installation of an Mk 15-5 bomb sight. The sight is rubber mounted. It is located directly in front of the bomber's seat.

The sighting window is provided with two metal covers. The outside cover is retractable into the nose by operating the retracting mechanism located in the compartment at the top of the window. The inside cover has a quick release locking arrangement. It is held down by eight locks, which can be released simultaneously by operating the locking mechanism in the center of the cover. This cover can be removed with the bomb sight in place.

A handhole, with a cover removable on the inside, is located immediately to the right of the sighting window in the nose of the airplane. The handhole permits the bomber to clean the outside of the window during flight. The instrument panel is located on the right-hand side of the sighting window.

(4) CONTROLS.

(a) GENERAL.

1. The controls are designed to permit either the bomber or the pilot to release bombs, either electrically or manually. The bomber sets up the electrical circuits and controls the selection of bombs to be released electrically, and the arming of the bomb fuses. The pilot (or co-pilot) has control of the release of torpedoes. He can release them singly or together, electrically, or both together, manually.

2. Bombs and torpedoes are normally released electrically. Bomb fuses are normally armed electrically. The fuses of bombs carried on the Mk 42 racks can be armed either electrically or manually.

3. The emergency salvo release controls are installed both in the bomber's and in the pilot's compartments. Those in the bomber's compartment serve only for the salvo release of bombs. Those in the pilot's compartment serve for the salvo release of either bombs or torpedoes. The emergency salvo release will release bombs with fuses either armed or safe.

4. The bomber's electrical control switch panel is located in the left-hand forward corner of the bomber's compartment. *(See figures 59 and 60.)*

5. The bomber's firing key (NAF 1174) is stowed in a canvas bag in the right-hand forward corner of the bomber's compartment.

6. The intervalometer type 2-1, together with the intervalometer electrical panel, is mounted on the left-hand side of the bomber's compartment.

7. The bomb sight Mk 15-5 is installed in the front of the bomber's compartment.

8. The bomber's emergency release handles and manual arming handles are located on each side of the sighting window. There are two sets of these controls, each consisting of two handles. The set on the left-hand side controls the bomb racks on left-hand side of the airplane. That on the right-hand side controls the bomb racks on the right-hand side of the airplane.

9. The pilot's switch panel has three switches and a firing key receptacle for use in releasing bombs or torpedoes.

10. The pilot's firing key (NAF1174) is stowed below the pilot's instrument panel, and forward of the pilot's right rudder pedal.

11. The pilot's emergency release handles are mounted just below the pilot's instrument panel, one on each side of the center line.

(b) ARMING AND RELEASE SYSTEM.

1. ELECTRICAL CONTROL.

a. Switches on the bomber's switch panel provide for arming the fuses on either the Mk 42 bomb racks or on the Mk 51-7 bomb racks.

b. The bomber has the choice of two methods of electrical release—automatic and manual electric. In automatic release the bomb sight will initiate the electrical impulse, which starts the functioning of the release system. The manual electric release requires that the bomber operate his firing key to provide the electrical impulse.

c. The automatic and the manual electric release each will release bombs selectively (one bomb or a salvo of several bombs released by one electrical impulse) or in train (a series of bombs released by one electrical impulse, which activates the intervalometer.)

d. Switches on the bomber's switch panel permit the bomber to set up the circuit, so that one or more bombs will be released by any of the methods described above.

e. The intervalometer Mk 2-1 is a multi-wire intervalometer. Its electrical mechanism provides for the release of bombs in train. The bombs are released successively so that their points of impact will be separated by that number of feet set by the bomber on the intervalometer. *(See figure 61.)*

f. The intervalometer assembly in addition to the intervalometer, includes electrical switches and jacks mounted on an intervalometer panel and electrical wiring contained in the intervalometer box.

g. Four toggle switches are mounted on the upper left-hand corner of the intervalometer panel. From the left to right these control the circuits from the intervalometer to:

Port outboard internal Mk 51-7 bomb rack.

Port inboard internal Mk 51-7 bomb rack.

Starboard inboard internal Mk 51-7 bomb rack.

Starboard outboard internal Mk 51-7 bomb rack.

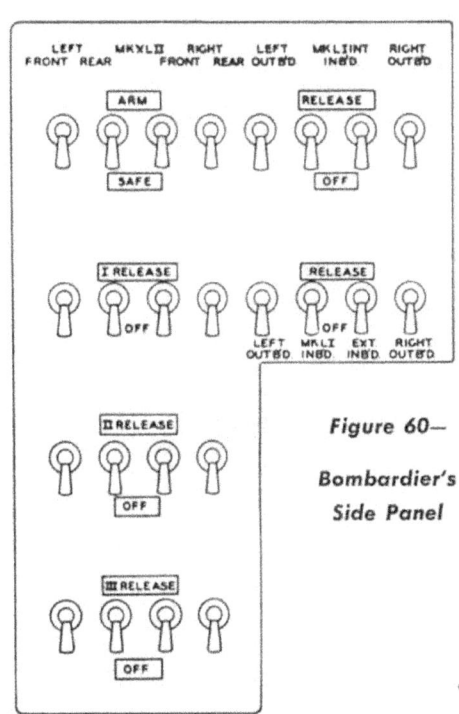

Figure 60—Bombardier's Side Panel

Figure 59—Bombardier's Front Panel

Section V

AN 01-5MA-1

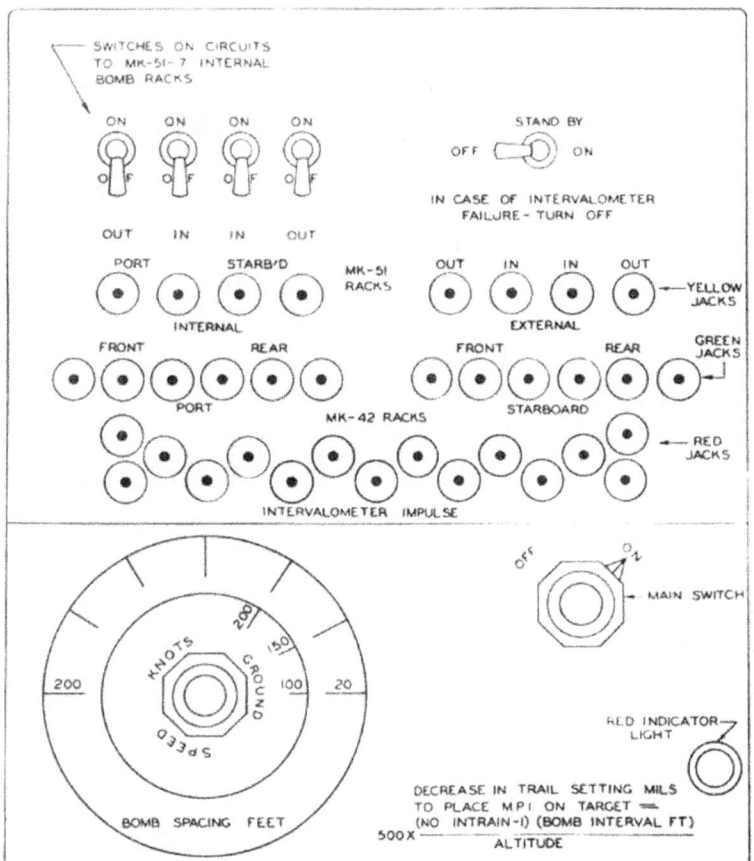

Figure 61—

Intervalometer Panel

Figure 62—

Bombardier's
Instrument Panel

1. Outside Air Temperature Indicator
2. Lateral Inclinometer
3. Air Speed Indicator
4. Altimeter

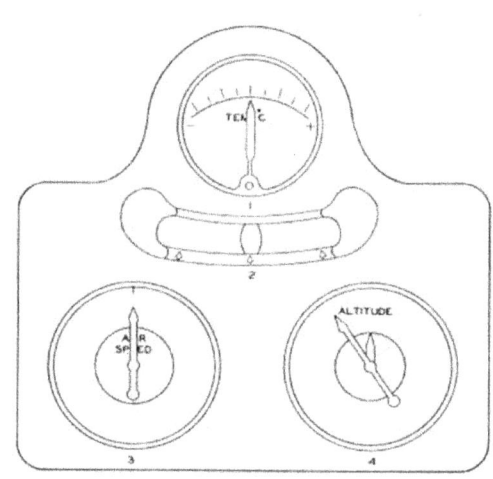

90

Section V
Paragraph 4

AN 01-5MA-1

Electric circuits from the intervalometer proper to these racks are permanently installed, and to release one or more bombs from these racks by the intervalometer, it is only necessary to move the proper switches to the "ON" position.

h. Three sets of colored jacks are mounted on the intervalometer panel.

i. Eight yellow jacks are for the eight Mk 51-7 bomb racks. The panel is marked, indicating jack and its rack.

j. Twelve green jacks are for the 12 bomb positions on the Mk 42 bomb racks. The panel is marked, indicating jacks and their respective racks.

k. Fifteen red jacks are for the intervalometer impulses. These are not numbered, but operate in order as indicated below:

```
1    3    5    7    9    11    13    14
 2    4    6    8    10    12    15
```

l. By the use of plugs and jumper wires, any intervalometer impulse jack can be connected to any bomb rack jack, thus allowing the release of bombs by the intervalometer from any racks and in any order. If jumpers are connected to intervalometer impulse jacks Nos. 1, 2, 3, and 4, the toggle switches for Mk 51-7 internal racks should be set to the "OFF" position.

m. In the upper right-hand corner of the intervalometer panel there is a stand-by switch. This switch is "ON" for normal operation of the intervalometer. In case of intervalometer failure, the switch is turned to the "OFF" position. This breaks the electrical circuit through the intervalometer, and reconnects the circuit from the firing key through the rack selector switches to the bomb racks.

n. On the right-hand side of the face of the intervalometer there is a master switch marked "OFF" and "ON." This switch must be "ON" for operation of the intervalometer. A red indicator light is below and to the right of the switch. The indicator light shows when the electrical circuits are routed through the intervalometer and are energized.

o. On the lower left-hand side of the face of the intervalometer there are two concentric dials—the outer graduated in "Bomb Spacing Feet" from 20 to 200, and the inner graduated in "Ground Speed Knots" from 100 to 200. A knob for turning the inner dial is centered on the dial. By setting the line on the inner dial representing the ground speed of the airplane to the line on the outer dial representing the bomb spacing desired, the intervalometer is set to send out electrical impulses so spaced that the impacts of the bombs released will be the desired distance apart.

p. After the proper switches are operated and the ground speed dial is set, the intervalometer operation will be activated either by a pressure of the firing key or by the bomb sight.

q. The pilot's switch panel has three switches which affect bomb and torpedo release. Two of these switches are for torpedo selection. Operating these will connect the circuit to either or both torpedo racks, so that the pilot can release the torpedoes. This operation of releasing torpedoes is under the pilot's control and is independent of the bomber. There is a double throw switch (with a red guard) marked "BOMB-TORPEDO." In the "BOMB" position, this switch sets up a circuit so that bombs can be released by the pilot, and cuts the bomber's firing key receptacle out of the circuit. In the "TORPEDO" position, the switch sets up a circuit so that torpedoes can be released by the pilot.

r. The pilot's switch panel has a receptacle for the pilot's firing key (NAF 1174). With the switches in proper position as explained above, operating the pilot's firing key will release either or both torpedoes.

s. With the "BOMB-TORPEDO" switch set to the "BOMB" position, the pilot can release bombs electrically, but only from the racks selected, and in the condition of fuse arming or safety, as set up by the bomber on his switch panel.

INTERVALOMETER TROUBLES.

TROUBLE	CAUSE	REMEDY
Intervalometer fails to operate.	Electrical trouble in intervalometer.	Temporary remedy: Turn intervalometer main switch and stand-by switch to "OFF" positions. Operate bombing system without intervalometer. Permanent remedy: Remove and replace intervalometer. Have faulty intervalometer repaired.

1. Pilot's Firing Key Stowage
2. Bomb and Torpedo Release Handles

Figure 63—Pilot's Emergency Bomb and Torpedo Release Handles

2. MANUAL CONTROL.

(See figure 63.)

a. The bomber's manual controls consist of two units—one left-hand for bomb racks on left side of airplane, and one right-hand for bomb racks on right side of airplane. Each unit has two handles connected by flexible cables to the bomb racks. The emergency release handle is marked "EMERGENCY RELEASE MK 42 MK 51." Pulling this handle will release all bombs on its side of the airplane in salvo. The Mk 42 safe and arming handle has two positions, marked "SAFE" and "MK 42 ARMED." Pulling this handle to the armed position will arm the fuses of bombs carried on the Mk 42 racks. This handle is independent of the electrical fusing system.

b. The pilot's emergency release controls have two handles, mounted just below the pilot's instrument panel, one left-hand and one right-hand of the center line. The left-hand handle controls bombs or torpedo on left side of airplane and the right-hand handle controls bombs or torpedo on right side of airplane. The handle is connected by flexible cable and a cable splice plate to the bomber's emergency release cable. A pull on the pilot's emergency handle will operate the emergency release system.

c. A two inch pull on the cable is required to release the bombs. In adjusting the cables, turn the turnbuckles just enough to remove the slack in the cables and no more. Check to see that the emergency release handle is in the closed position after the cables have been adjusted. Too great a tension on the cables may result in dropping bombs inadvertently.

d. The manual control system for the Mk 42 racks remains in the airplane at all times, even when the Mk 42 racks are removed.

3. BOMBING SYSTEM TROUBLES.

TROUBLE	CAUSE	REMEDY
Bomb rack fails to release.	If bomb cannot be released manually at rack, bent, broken or rusted bomb rack.	Remove rack and replace.
	If bomb can be released manually at rack, broken or stuck salvo release cable.	Check cable. Replace broken section. Replace broken or warped pulley or bracket causing sticking.
	Electrical circuit interrupted.	Check switches and fuses. If this does not correct trouble, then check circuit for continuity. Correct any faults discovered.

(c) BOMBER'S INSTRUMENT PANEL.
(See figure 62.)

The panel is mounted in the right-hand forward corner of the bomber's compartment. Mounted on it are a free air thermometer, a lateral inclinometer, an air speed indicator and an altimeter.

(5) TORPEDO TRAINING CAMERA.—Provision is made for the installation of a torpedo training camera immediately forward of station 1.66 on top of the pilot's enclosure.

★ ★ ★

Appendix 1 of this publication shall not be carried in aircraft on combat missions or when there is a reasonable chance of its falling into the hands of the enemy.

Appendix 1

AN 01-5MA-1

APPENDIX 1
FLIGHT OPERATING CHARTS, TABLES CURVES AND DIAGRAMS

TAKE-OFF, CLIMB & LANDING CHART

AIRCRAFT MODEL(S): PBY-5A
ENGINE MODEL(S): R-1830-92

TAKE-OFF DISTANCE (FEET)

GROSS WEIGHT LB.	HEAD WIND M.P.H.	HEAD WIND KTS.	HARD SURFACE RUNWAY — AT SEA LEVEL GROUND RUN	HARD SURFACE RUNWAY — AT SEA LEVEL TO CLEAR 50' OBJ.	AT 3000 FEET GROUND RUN	AT 3000 FEET TO CLEAR 50' OBJ.	AT 6000 FEET GROUND RUN	AT 6000 FEET TO CLEAR 50' OBJ.	SOD-TURF RUNWAY — AT SEA LEVEL GROUND RUN	AT SEA LEVEL TO CLEAR 50' OBJ.	AT 3000 FEET GROUND RUN	AT 3000 FEET TO CLEAR 50' OBJ.	AT 6000 FEET GROUND RUN	AT 6000 FEET TO CLEAR 50' OBJ.	SOFT SURFACE RUNWAY — AT SEA LEVEL GROUND RUN	AT SEA LEVEL TO CLEAR 50' OBJ.	AT 3000 FEET GROUND RUN	AT 3000 FEET TO CLEAR 50' OBJ.	AT 6000 FEET GROUND RUN	AT 6000 FEET TO CLEAR 50' OBJ.
28,000	0	0	1100	2160	1290	2460	1550	2960	1180	2240	1400	2570	1670	3100	1450	2510	1730	2970	2110	3540
	12	10	820	1710	980	1965	1180	2375	870	1760	1070	2045	1270	2465	1080	1970	1320	2295	1590	2805
	23	20	660	1410	780	1610	950	1970	690	1445	840	1670	1040	2040	870	1605	1040	1870	1290	2330
	35	30	510	1150	620	1325	760	1615	550	1195	670	1375	820	1675	680	1320	830	1535	1040	1975
31,000	0	0	1410	2800	1640	3185	1930	3850	1540	2950	1760	3305	2140	4050	1940	3330	2230	3855	2800	4800
	12	10	1080	2225	1280	2560	1490	3105	1160	2335	1350	2650	1650	3265	1480	2625	1750	3050	2220	3835
	23	20	850	1840	1000	2120	1160	2530	920	1925	1080	2190	1290	2660	1170	2160	1410	2480	1740	3110
	35	30	680	1510	810	1720	980	2030	740	1570	860	1870	1080	2230	930	1760	1120	2110	1450	2660
34,000	0	0	1750	3590	2060	4120	2420	5065	1950	3800	2250	4250	2750	5335	2640	4400	3080	5180	3950	5995
	12	10	1340	2905	1590	3320	1800	4120	1580	3065	1770	3430	2280	4370	2020	3585	2380	4110	3080	5310
	23	20	1070	2430	1240	2710	1540	3430	1330	2510	1500	2800	1750	3640	1610	2920	1830	3330	2510	4400
	35	30	860	1980	1050	2240	1220	2820	1120	2070	1220	2320	1440	2840	1290	2410	1500	2720	1980	3580

NOTE: INCREASE CHART DISTANCES AS FOLLOWS: 75°F + 10%; 100°F + 20%; 125°F + 30%; 150°F + 40%. OPTIMUM TAKE-OFF WITH 2700 RPM, 48 IN. HG., 0 DEG. FLAPS IS 80% OF CHART VALUES

DATA AS OF OCT. 1944 BASED ON: CALCULATIONS

CLIMB DATA

GROSS WEIGHT LB.	AT SEA LEVEL BEST I.A.S. MPH	KTS	RATE OF CLIMB F.P.M.	GAL. OF FUEL USED	AT 5000 FEET BEST I.A.S. MPH	KTS	RATE OF CLIMB F.P.M.	FROM SEA LEVEL TIME MIN.	FUEL USED	AT 10,000 FEET BEST I.A.S. MPH	KTS	RATE OF CLIMB F.P.M.	FROM SEA LEVEL TIME MIN.	FUEL USED	AT 15,000 FEET BEST I.A.S. MPH	KTS	RATE OF CLIMB F.P.M.	FROM SEA LEVEL TIME MIN.	FUEL USED	AT 20,000 FEET BEST I.A.S. MPH	KTS	RATE OF CLIMB F.P.M.	FROM SEA LEVEL TIME MIN.	FUEL USED
28,000	89	77	890	50	89	77	835	6.0		89	77	680	12.2	100	89	77	425	21.2	130	89	77	170	37.9	195
31,000	93	81	740	50	93	81	690	7.25		93	81	530	14.9	110	93	81	280	27.3	155					
34,000	98	85	610	50	98	85	560	8.9		98	85	400	18.5	120	98	85	150	36.7	190					

POWER PLANT SETTINGS (DETAILS ON FIG. 38 SECTION 1.1.2)
DATA AS OF OCT. 1944 BASED ON: CALCULATIONS

FUEL USED (U.S. GAL.) INCLUDES WARM-UP & TAKE-OFF ALLOWANCE

LANDING DISTANCE (FEET)

GROSS WEIGHT LB.	BEST IAS APPROACH POWER OFF MPH	KTS	POWER ON MPH	KTS	HARD DRY SURFACE — AT SEA LEVEL GROUND ROLL	TO CLEAR 50' OBJ.	AT 3000 FEET GROUND ROLL	TO CLEAR 50' OBJ.	AT 6000 FEET GROUND ROLL	TO CLEAR 50' OBJ.	FIRM DRY SOD — AT SEA LEVEL GROUND ROLL	TO CLEAR 50' OBJ.	AT 3000 FEET GROUND ROLL	TO CLEAR 50' OBJ.	AT 6000 FEET GROUND ROLL	TO CLEAR 50' OBJ.	WET OR SLIPPERY — AT SEA LEVEL GROUND ROLL	TO CLEAR 50' OBJ.	AT 3000 FEET GROUND ROLL	TO CLEAR 50' OBJ.	AT 6000 FEET GROUND ROLL	TO CLEAR 50' OBJ.
26,000	83	72	77	67	980	2250	1080	2410	1170	2590	1150	2415	1250	2590	1370	2780	3300	5160	4260	5600	4680	6090
34,000	95	82	88	76	1290	2800	1410	3000	1540	3240	1500	3020	1650	3160	1800	3500	4580	6100	5000	6600	5580	7180

DATA AS OF OCT. 1944 BASED ONLY CALCULATIONS

OPTIMUM LANDING IS 80% OF CHART VALUES

REMARKS:
NOTE: TO DETERMINE FUEL CONSUMPTION IN BRITISH IMPERIAL GALLONS, MULTIPLY BY 10, THEN DIVIDE BY 12

LEGEND
I.A.S. — INDICATED AIRSPEED
M.P.H. — MILES PER HOUR
KTS. — KNOTS
F.P.M. — FEET PER MINUTE

Figure 64—Take-Off, Climb and Landing Chart

Appendix 1 of this publication shall not be carried in aircraft on combat missions or when there is a reasonable chance of its falling into the hands of the enemy.

AN 01-5MA-1

Appendix I

AIRCRAFT MODEL(S): PBY-5A					FLIGHT OPERATION INSTRUCTION CHART				EXTERNAL LOAD ITEMS: NONE			
ENGINE(S): R-1830-92					CHART WEIGHT LIMITS: 32,000 to 34,000 POUNDS				NUMBER OF ENGINES OPERATING: 2			

NOTES: COLUMN I IS FOR EMERGENCY HIGH SPEED CRUISING ONLY. COLUMNS II, III, IV AND V GIVE PROGRESSIVE INCREASE IN RANGE AT A SACRIFICE IN SPEED. AIR MILES PER GALLON (MI./GAL.) (NO WIND), GALLONS PER HR. (G.P.H.) AND TRUE AIRSPEED (T.A.S.) ARE APPROXIMATE VALUES FOR REFERENCE. RANGE VALUES ARE FOR AN AVERAGE AIRPLANE FLYING ALONE (NO WIND). TO OBTAIN BRITISH IMPERIAL GAL. (OR G.P.H.) MULTIPLY U.S.GAL (OR G.P.H.) BY 10 THEN DIVIDE BY 12.

INSTRUCTIONS FOR USING CHART: SELECT FIGURE IN FUEL COLUMN EQUAL TO OR LESS THAN AMOUNT OF FUEL TO BE USED FOR CRUISING. MOVE HORIZONTALLY TO RIGHT OR LEFT AND SELECT RANGE VALUE EQUAL TO OR GREATER THAN THE STATUTE OR NAUTICAL AIR MILES TO BE FLOWN. VERTICALLY BELOW AND OPPOSITE (ALT.) READ RPM, MANIFOLD PRESSURE DESIRED CRUISING ALTITUDE (ALT.) READ RPM, MANIFOLD PRESSURE (M.P.) AND MIXTURE SETTING REQUIRED.

Figure 65—Flight Operation Instruction Chart

RED FIGURES ARE PRELIMINARY DATA, SUBJECT TO REVISION AFTER FLIGHT CHECK

LEGEND:
ALT. : PRESSURE ALTITUDE
M.P. : MANIFOLD PRESSURE
G.P.H. : U.S. GAL. PER HOUR
T.A.S. : TRUE AIRSPEED
KTS. : KNOTS
S.L. : SEA LEVEL

R.P.M. : FULL RICH
A.R. : AUTO-RICH
A.L. : AUTO-LEAN
C.L. : CRUISING LEAN
M.L. : MANUAL LEAN
F.T. : FULL THROTTLE

95

Appendix I of this publication shall not be carried in aircraft on combat missions or when there is a reasonable chance of its falling into the hands of the enemy.

Appendix I

AN 01-5MA-1

CRUISING CHART

PRESSURE ALTITUDE FEET	MAXIMUM CRUISE 140 BMEP – AUTO LEAN		INTERMEDIATE CRUISE 140 BMEP – AUTO LEAN		MIN. SPEC. CONSUMPTION 140 BMEP – AUTO LEAN	
	RPM	MAN. PRES. "HG. (ABS)	RPM	MAN. PRES. "HG. (ABS)	RPM	MAN. PRES. "HG. (ABS)
1,000	2170	33.5	1950	33.5	1610	33.0
4,000	2170	32.0	1950	32.0	1610	32.0
7,000	2170	31.0	1950	31.0	1650	F.T.*
10,000	2170	30.5	2050**	F.T.*	**	
13,000	2275**	F.T.*	**		**	

* FULL THROTTLE ALTITUDE VARIES WITH OPERATING CONDITIONS.
** INCREASE RPM TO MAINTAIN POWER (140 BMEP NO LONGER AVAILABLE)

Figure 66—Cruising Chart

Appendix I of this publication shall not be carried in aircraft on combat missions or when there is a reasonable chance of its falling into the hands of the enemy.

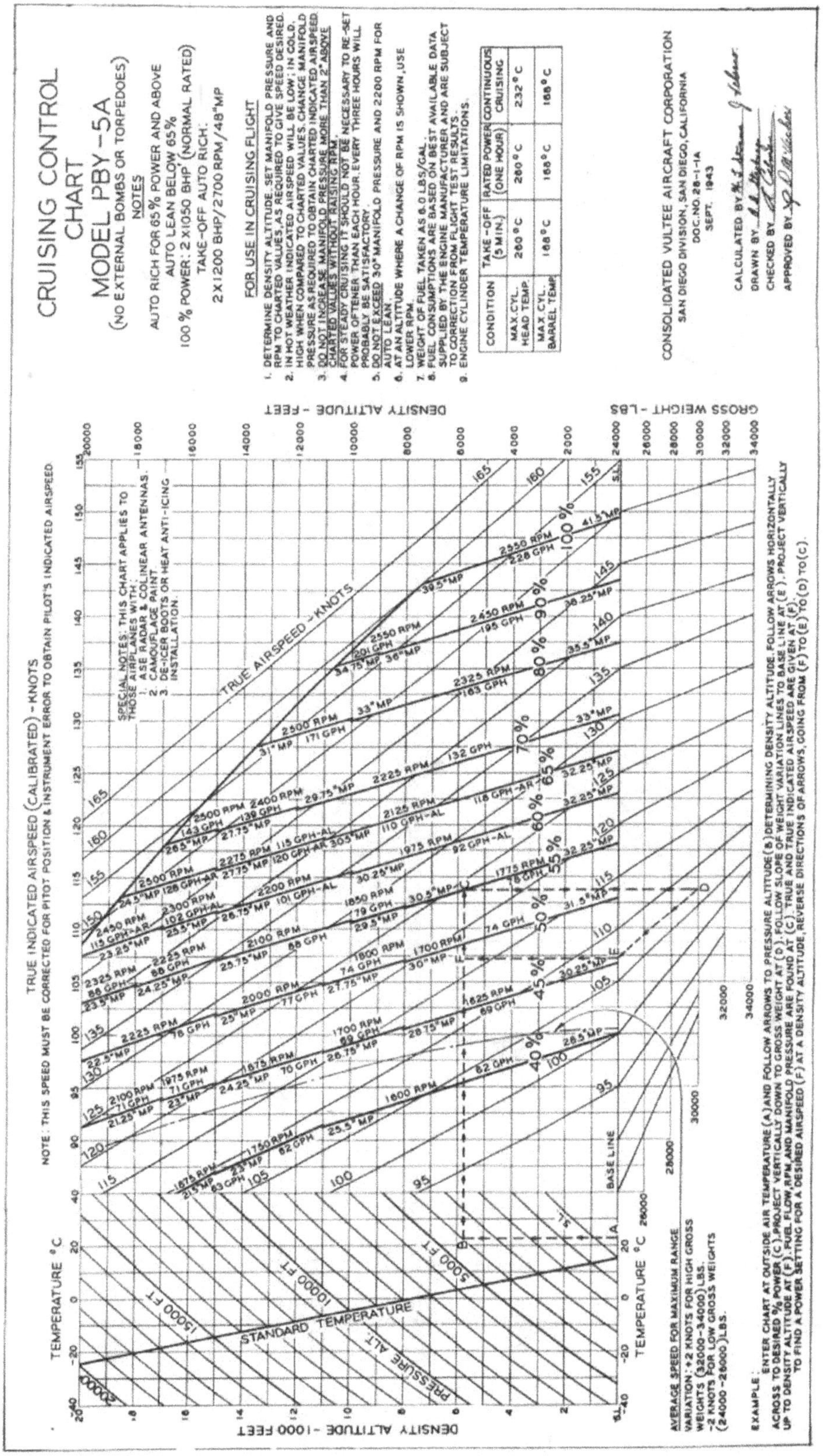

RESTRICTED
AN 01-5MA-1

Appendix I

Figure 67—Cruising Control Chart

Appendix I of this publication shall not be carried in aircraft on combat missions or when there is a reasonable chance of its falling into the hands of the enemy.

Appendix I

AN 01-5MA-1

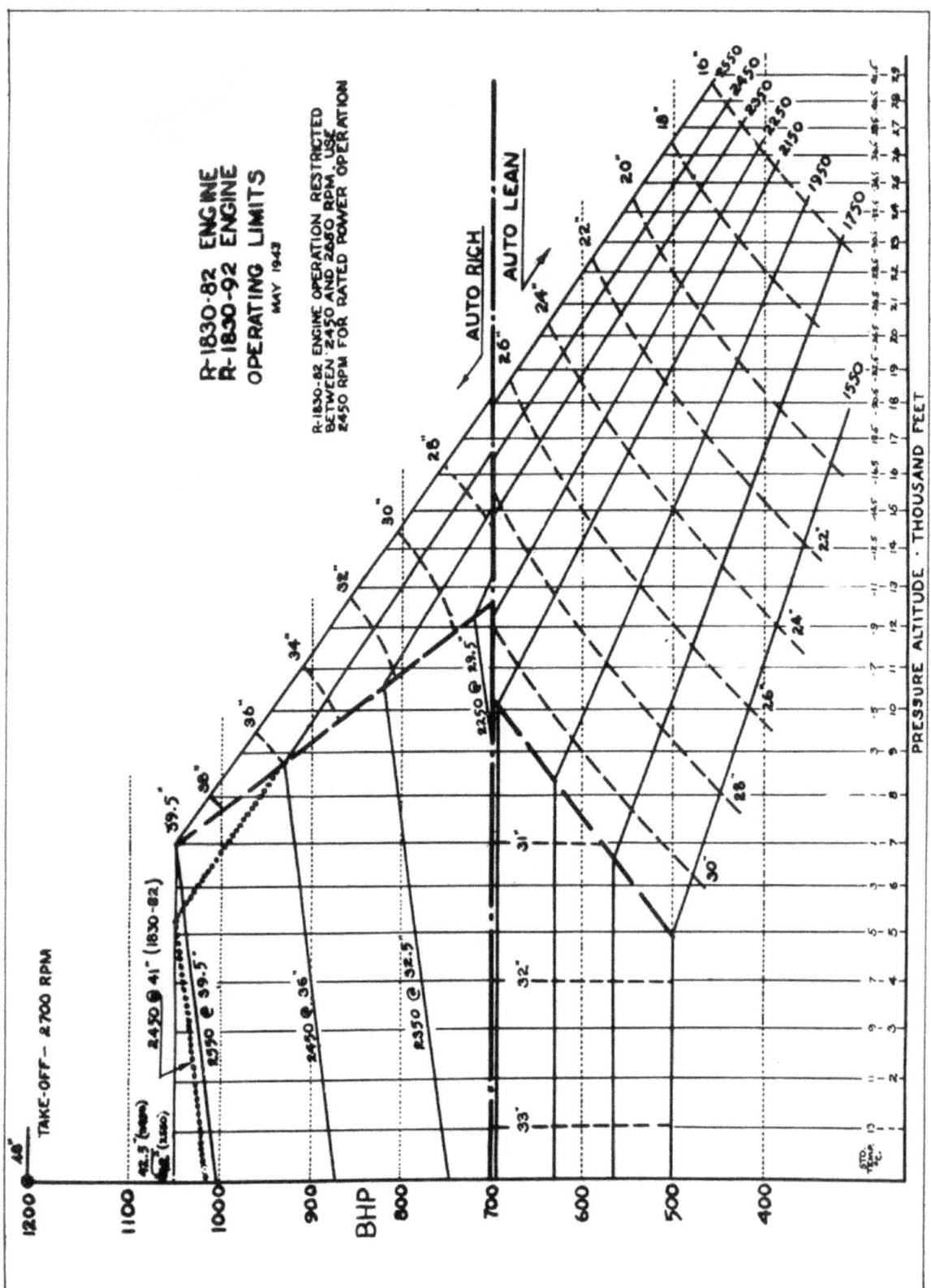

Figure 68—Engine Calibration Curve

©2007-2010 Periscope Film LLC
All Rights Reserved
ISBN #978-1-935327-94-3   1-935327-94-1
www.PeriscopeFilm.com

Aircraft At War DVD Series

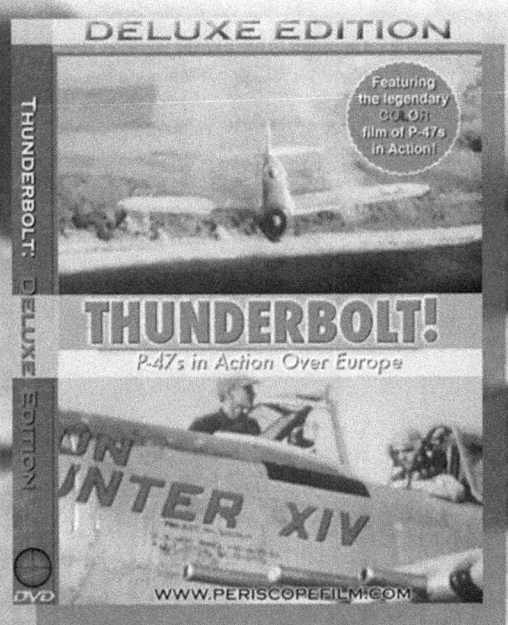
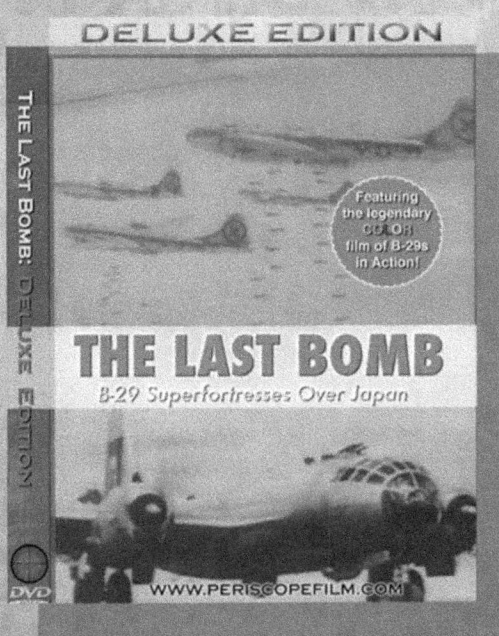
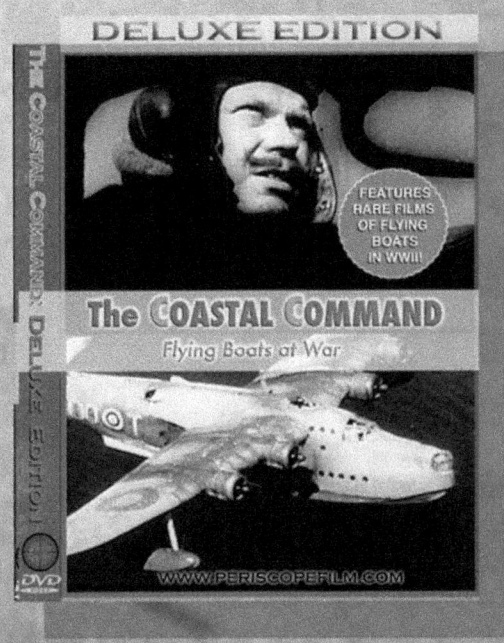

Now Available!

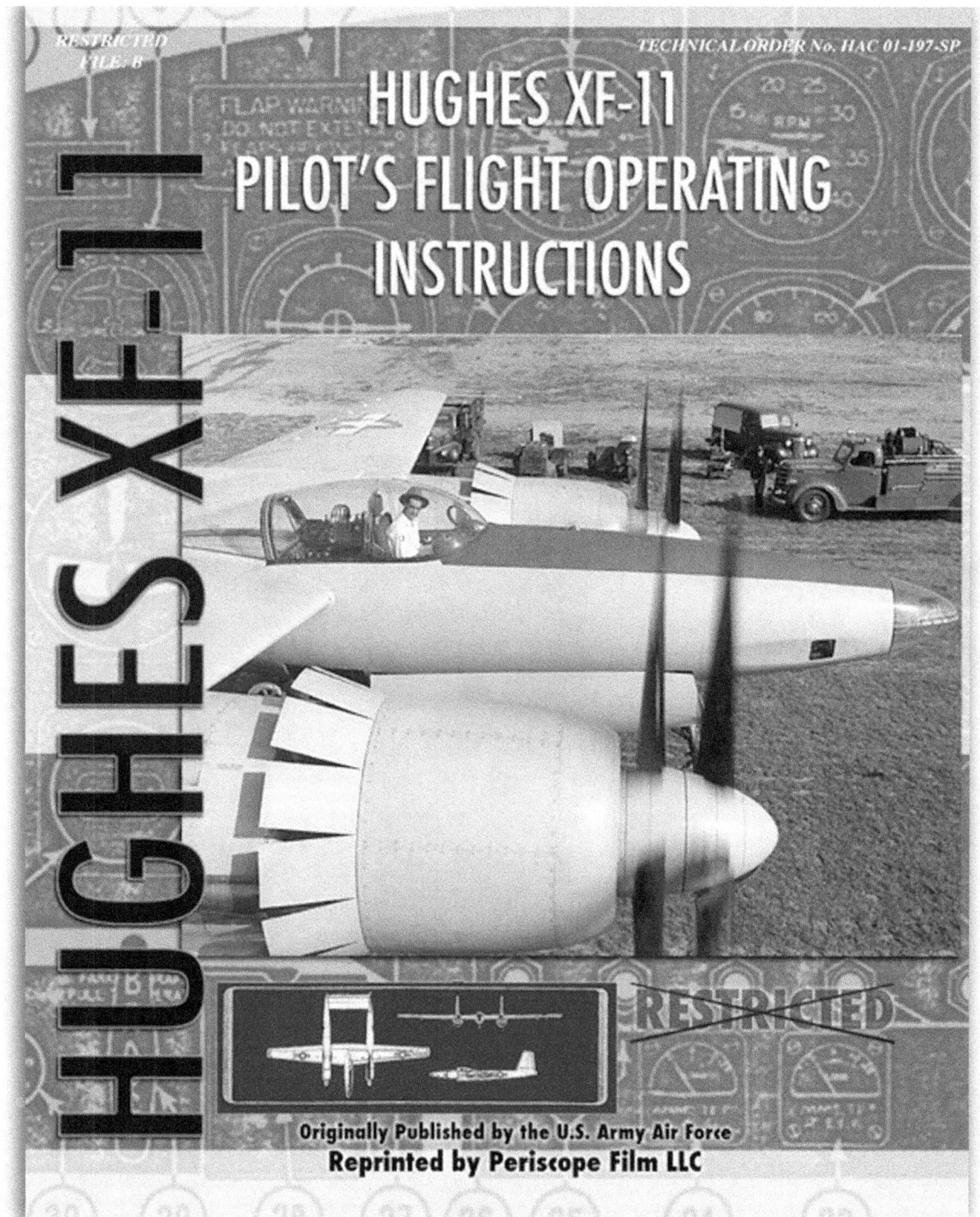

NOW AVAILABLE!

SPRUCE GOOSE
HUGHES FLYING BOAT MANUAL

Originally Published by the War Department
Reprinted by Periscope Film LLC

RESTRICTED

NOW AVAILABLE!

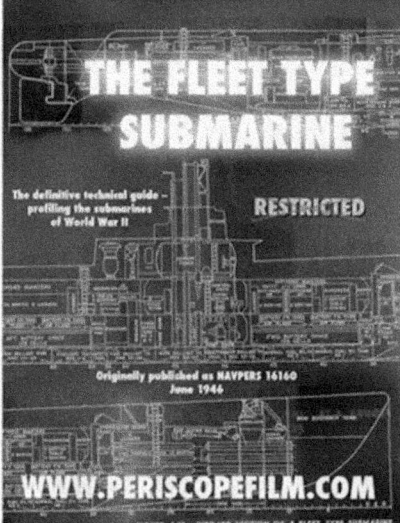

ALSO NOW AVAILABLE FROM PERISCOPEFILM.COM

THE CLASSIC 1915 TROLLEY CAR AND INTERURBAN RAILWAY BOOK

ELECTRIC RAILWAY ENGINEERING

By Francis H. Doane, A.M.B.

REPRINTED BY PERISCOPEFILM.COM

©2010 PERISCOPE FILM LLC
ALL RIGHTS RESERVED
ISBN 978-1-935700-18-0
WWW.PERISCOPEFILM.COM

www.ingramcontent.com/pod-product-compliance
Lightning Source LLC
Chambersburg PA
CBHW080448170426
43196CB00016B/2724